The Laws of Candy by John Ford & Philip Massinger

The play was originally attributed to, and published in, the folios of John Fletcher & Francis Beaumont but modern analysis and scholarship has defined the primary author as John Ford. There is also some evidence that the surviving play was reworked by Philip Massinger.

John Ford was born in 1586 in Ilsington, in Devon and baptizes on April 17th.

Details of his life are scare and some have a variance of truth about them. By 1602 Ford, had by most accounts, been admitted to Middle Temple in London, a prestigious law school but also a centre for literary and dramatic pursuits. In 1606 Ford was expelled due to his financial problems. He then wrote and had published two poems Fame's Memorial and Honour Triumphant. Two years later he was back at Middle Temple and would remain there until at least 1617.

His initial forays into playwriting began with other more senior and well-known collaborators such as Thomas Dekker, John Webster, and William Rowley. It is difficult to distinguish the share of the writing amongst them but certainly his themes, style, rhythm and language are at least an influence and undoubtedly grew with each production.

From about 1627 to 1638 Ford wrote plays by himself, mostly for private theatres and his outstanding reputation, is set mainly with his first four plays in which he was the sole author. Of these, 'Tis Pity She's a Whore is the most powerful.

Ford's austerely powerful themes are set off by subplots with minor characters and perhaps not the greatest of comedy, but together they outline him as the most important tragedian of the reign of King Charles I (1625–49).

Philip Massinger was baptized at St. Thomas's in Salisbury on November 24th, 1583.

Massinger is described in his matriculation entry at St. Alban Hall, Oxford (1602), as the son of a gentleman. His father, who had also been educated there, was a member of parliament, and attached to the household of Henry Herbert, 2nd Earl of Pembroke. The Earl was later seen as a potential patron for Massinger.

He left Oxford in 1606 without a degree. His father had died in 1603, and accounts suggest that Massinger was left with no financial support this, together with rumours that he had converted to Catholicism, meant the next stage of his career needed to provide an income.

Massinger went to London to make his living as a dramatist, but he is only recorded as author some fifteen years later, when The Virgin Martyr (1621) is given as the work of Massinger and Thomas Dekker.

During those early years as a playwright he wrote for the Elizabethan stage entrepreneur, Philip Henslowe. It was a difficult existence. Poverty was always close and there was constant pleading for advance payments on forthcoming works merely to survive.

After Henslowe died in 1616 Massinger and John Fletcher began to write primarily for the King's Men and Massinger would write regularly for them until his death.

The tone of the dedications in later plays suggests evidence of his continued poverty. In the preface of The Maid of Honour (1632) he wrote, addressing Sir Francis Foljambe and Sir Thomas Bland: "I had not to this time subsisted, but that I was supported by your frequent courtesies and favours."

The prologue to The Guardian (1633) refers to two unsuccessful plays and two years of silence, when the author feared he had lost popular favour although, from the little evidence that survives, it also seems he had involved some of his plays with political characters which would have cast shadows upon England's alliances.

Philip Massinger died suddenly at his house near the Globe Theatre on March 17th, 1640. He was buried the next day in the churchyard of St. Saviour's, Southwark, on March 18th, 1640. In the entry in the parish register he is described as a "stranger," which, however, implies nothing more than that he belonged to another parish.

Index of Contents

DRAMATIS PERSONAE
MEN
Cassilanes, General of Candy.
Antinous, Son to Cassilanes, and his Competitor.
Fernando, a Venetian Captain, Servant to Annophel.
Philander, Prince of Cyprus, passionately in love with Erota.
Gonzalo, An ambitious Politick Lord of Venice.

Gaspero, Secretary of State.
Melitus, a Gentleman of Candy.
Arcanes, a noble Souldier, Friend to Cassilanes.
Decius, Friend to Antinous.
Porphycio   }
Possenne   } Senators.
Paolo Michael, Venetian Ambassadour.
Mochingo, an ignorant Servant to Erota.
Gentlemen.
Souldiers.
Servants.
WOMEN
Erota, a Princess, imperious, and of an overweaning Beauty.
Annophel, Daughter to Cassilanes.
Hyparcha, Attendant on the Princess Erota.

ACTUS PRIMUS

SCÆNA PRIMA

Enter **GASPERO**, and **MELITUS**

MELITUS
Sir, you're the very friend I wish'd to meet with,
I have a large discourse invites your ear
To be an Auditor.

GASPERO
And what concerns it?

MELITUS
The sadly thriving progress of the loves
Between my Lord, the Prince, and that great Lady,
Whose insolence, and never-yet-match'd Pride,
Can by no Character be well exprest,
But in her only name, the proud Erota.

GASPERO
Alas, Melitus, I should guess the best
Success your Prince could find from her, to be
As harsh as the event doth prove: but now
'Tis not a time to pity passionate griefs,
When a whole Kingdom in a manner lyes
Upon its Death-Bed bleeding.

MELITUS

Who can tell
Whether or no these plagues at once
Hang over this unhappy Land for her sake
That is a Monster in it?

GASPERO
Here's the misery
Of having a Child our Prince; else I presume
The bold Venetians had not dar'd to attempt
So bloody an invasion.

MELITUS
Yet I wonder
Why (Master Secretary) still the Senate
So almost superstitiously adores
Gonzalo, the Venetian Lord, considering
The outrage of his Countrymen—

GASPERO
The Senate
Is wise, and therein just, for this Gonzalo,
Upon a Massacre performed at Sea
By the Admiral of Venice, on a Merchant
Of Candy, when the cause was to be heard
Before the Senate there, in open Court
Professed, that the cruelty the Admiral
Had shewed, deserved not only fine, but death;
For Candy then, and Venice were at peace:
Since when upon a motion in the Senate,
For Conquest of our Land, 'tis known for certain,
That only this Gonzalo dar'd to oppose it,
His reason was, because it too much savour'd
Of lawless and unjust ambition.
The Wars were scarce begun, but he (in fear
Of quarrels 'gainst his life) fled from his Country,
And hither came, where (to confirm his truth)
I know, (Melitus,) he out of his own store,
Hath monied Cassilanes the General.

MELITUS
What, without other pledges than Cassilanes
Bare promise of payment?

GASPERO
No, it may be
He has some petty Lordship to retire to;
But thus he hath done; now 'tis fit, Melitus,
The Senate should be thankful, otherwise

They should annihilate one of those Laws
For which this Kingdome is throughout the World
Unfollowed and admired.

MELITUS
What Laws are those, Sir?
Let me so much importune you.

GASPERO
You shall,
And they be worth your knowledge: briefly thus:
Who e'r he be that can detect apparently
Another of ingratitude, for any
Received Benefit, the Plaintiff may
Require the Offenders life; unless he please
Freely and willingly to grant remission.

MELITUS
By which strict Law, the Senate is in danger,
Should they neglect Gonzalo?

GASPERO
Right, the Law
Permits a like equality to Aliens,
As to a home-bred Patriot.

MELITUS
Pray Sir, the other?

GASPERO
Know, Melitus,
The elder Cretans flourished many years,
In War, in Peace unparallel'd, and they
(To spur heroic Spirits on to Vertue)
Enacted that what man so ere he were,
Did noblest in the field against his enemy,
So by the general voice approv'd, and known,
Might at his home-return, make his demand
For satisfaction, and reward.

MELITUS
They are
Both famous Laws indeed.

[Enter a **MESSENGER**

MESSENGER
Master Secretary,

The Senate is about to sit, and crave
Your presence.

GASPERO
What, so suddenly?

MESSENGER
These Letters
Will shew the causes why.

GASPERO
Heaven, thou art great,
And worthy to be thanked!

MELITUS
Your countenance, Sir,
Doth promise some good tidings.

GASPERO
O the best
And happiest for this land that e'r was told!
All the Venetian Forces are defeated.

MELITUS
How, Sir?

GASPERO
And what doth add some delight more,
There is amongst the Souldiers a contention
Who shall be the triumpher, and it stands
Doubtful between a Father and his Son,
Old Cassilanes, and young Antinous.

MELITUS
Why may not both demand it?

GASPERO
The Law denies it,
But where the Souldiers do not all consent,
The Parties in contention, are refer'd
To plead before the Senate; and from them
Upon an open audience to be judg'd
The Chief, and then to make demands.

MELITUS
You ravish me
With wonder and delight.

GASPERO
Come; as we walk,
I shall more fully inform you.

[Exeunt.

SCÆNA SECUNDA

Enter **CASSILANES, ARCANES, ANTINOUS**, and **DECIUS**.

CASSILANES
Admit no Souldier near us till the Senate
Have took their places.

ARCANES
You are obey'd, my Lord.

ANTINOUS
Decius, fall off.

DECIUS
I shall.

CASSILANES
Give leave Arcanes:
Young man, come nearer to me: who am I?

ANTINOUS
It were a sin against the piety
Of filial duty, if I should forget
The debt I owe my Father on my knee:
Your pleasure?

CASSILANES
What, so low? canst thou find joints,
Yet be an Elephant? Antinous, rise;
Thou wilt belye opinion, and rebate
The ambition of thy gallantry, that they
Whose confidence thou hast bewitch'd, should see
Their little God of War, kneel to his Father,
Though in my hand I did grasp Thunder.

ANTINOUS
Sir,
For proof that I acknowledge you the Author
Of giving me my Birth, I have discharg'd

A part of my Obedience. But if now
You should (as cruel fathers do) proclaim
Your right, and Tyrant-like usurp the glory
Of my peculiar honours, not deriv'd
From successary, but purchas'd with my bloud,
Then I must stand first Champion for my self
Against all interposers.

CASSILANES
Boldly urg'd,
And proudly, I could love thee, did not anger
Consult with just disdain, in open language
To call thee most ungrateful. Say freely,
Wilt thou resign the flatteries whereon
The reeling pillars of a popular breath
Have rais'd thy Giant-like conceit, to add
A suffrage to thy Fathers merit? speak.

ANTINOUS
Sir, hear me: were there not a Chronicle
Well pen'd by all their tongues, who can report
What they have seen you do; or had you not
Best in your own performance writ your self,
And been your own text, I would undertake
Alone, without the help of Art, or Character,
But only to recount your deeds in Arms,
And you should ever then be fam'd a President
Of living victory: But as you are
Great, and well worthy to be stiled Great,
It would betray a poverty of Spirit
In me to obstruct my fortunes, or descent,
If I should coward-like surrender up
The interest which the inheritance of your vertue
And mine own thrifty fate can claim in honour:
My Lord, of all the mass of Fame, which any
That wears a Sword, and hath but seen me fight,
Gives me, I will not share, nor yield one jot,
One tittle.

CASSILANES
Not to me?

ANTINOUS
You are my Father,
Yet not to you.

CASSILANES
Ambitious Boy, how dar'st thou

To tell me, that thou wilt contend?

ANTINOUS
Had I
Been slothful, and not follow'd you in all
The streights of death, you might have justly then
Reputed me a Bastard: 'tis a cruelty
More than to murther Innocents, to take
The life of my yet infant-honour from me.

CASSILANES
Antinous, look upon this badge of age,
Thy Father's grey-hair'd beard: full fifty years,
(And more than half of this, ere thou wert born)
I have been known a Souldier, in which time
I found no difference 'twixt War and Peace,
For War was Peace to me, and Peace was War.
Antinous, mark me well; there hath not liv'd
These fifty years a man whom Crete prefer'd
Before thy Father; let me boldly boast,
Thy Father, both for Discipline and Action
Hath so long been the first of all his Nation;
Now, canst thou think it honest, charitable,
Nay humane, being so young, my Son, my Child,
Begot, bred, taught by me, by me thy Father,
For one days service, and that on thy first,
To rob me of a glory which I fought for
A half of hundred years?

ANTINOUS
My case observes
Both equity and presidents; for Sir,
That very day whereon you got your Fame,
You took it from some other, who was then
Chief in repute, as you are now, and has been
Perhaps as many years deserving that
Which you gain'd in a day, as I have mine.

CASSILANES
But he was not my Father then, Antinous;
Thou leav'st out that.

ANTINOUS
Sir, had he been your Father,
He had been then immortal; for a Father
Heightens his reputation where his Son
Inherits it, as when you give us life,
Your life is not diminish'd but renew'd

In us when you are dead, and we are still
Your living Images.

CASSILANES
So be thou curs'd
In thy posterity, as I in thee,
Dishonourable Boy; O shall that Sun,
Which not a year yet since beheld me mounted
Upon a fiery Steed, waving my Sword,
And teaching this young Man to manage Arms,
That was a raw, fresh Novice in the feats
Of Chivalrie, shall that same Sun be witness
Against this Brat of his Ingratitude?
Who, to eclipse the light of my renown,
Can no way hope to get a noble Name,
But by the treading on his Father's Greatness;
Thou wilt not yield?

[Enter **ARCANES**

ANTINOUS
My life, but not the prize
My Sword hath purchas'd.

ARCANES
The Senate,
My Lord, are here at hand, and all the Souldiers
Begin to throng about them.

CASSILANES
Now, Arcanes, the—

ARCANES
What, Sir?

CASSILANES
Trifles will affront us; that
Fine fighting Stripling.

ARCANES
Let him have the shame on't;
'Please you withdraw on this side.

CASSILANES
My great heart
Was never quail'd before.

DECIUS

My Lord, be confident,
Let not your Father daunt you.

ARCANES
Decius, whither
Must I withdraw?

DECIUS
On this side.—See, the Souldiers
Attend your pleasure—courage, Sir; the Senate.

CASSILANES
Way for the Senate.

[Enter **PORPHYCIO, POSSENNE, GONZALO, GASPERO, SOULDIERS.**

My good Lords I know not
What tax of arrogance I may incurr,
Should I presume, though courted by your Favours,
To take a place amongst you; I had rather
Give proof of my unfeign'd humility
By force, though mean, yet more becoming place,
Than run the hazard of a doubtful censure.

POSSENNE
My Lord, your wisdom is both known and try'd;
We cannot rank you in a nobler Friendship
Than your great service to the State deserves.

PORPHYCIO
Will't please you, Sir?

[Enter **FERNANDO** with **SOULDIERS.**

GONZALO
What's here, my Lord Porphycio?
It must not be.

PORPHYCIO
My Lord, you are too modest.

GONZALO
It is no season to be troublesome,
Else—but I have done: your Lordships are observ'd.

GASPERO
Is the demandant ready?

ARCANES
He is ready.

GASPERO
Produce him then.

ARCANES
Before this sacred presence,
I, by a general consent, am made
The Souldiers voice, and to your gracious Wisedoms,
Present as chief in Arms, his Countries Champion,
Cassilanes.

DECIUS
Most reverend Lords, you hear the lesser number
Of those who have been Guardians to this Country,
Approve this Champion; I, in all their names,
Who fought for Candy, here present before you
The mightiest man in Arms, Antinous.
Speak fellow Souldiers.

SOULDIERS
Antinous, Antinous.

GASPERO
Stand by all, save the two Competitors.

POSSENNE
My Lords, how much your Countrey owes you both,
The due reward of your desertful glories
Must to Posterity remain: but yet
Since, by our Law, one only can make claim
To the proposed honours which you both
(It seems) have truly merited, take leave
Freely to plead your rights; we shall attend ye.

PORPHYCIO
Wherein priority of voice is granted,
Lord Cassilanes to you; for that your rare
And long experience in the Course of War,
As well doth challenge it as the best priviledge
Of Order and Civility, for that
You are your brave Opponents worthy Father.
Say, Country-men, are you content?

SOULDIERS
I, I.

CASSILANES

Right grave, right gracious Fathers; how unfit
It is for me, that all my life time have
Been practis'd in the School of Bloud, and Slaughter
To bandy words now in my lifes last farewel,
Your Wisedomes will consider; were there pitcht
Another, and another field, like that
Which, not yet three days since, this Arm hath scatter'd,
Defeated, and made nothing, then the man
That had a heart to think he could but follow
(For equal me he should not) through the lanes
Of danger and amazement, might in that
That only of but following me, be happy,
Reputed worthy to be made my Rival;
For 'tis not, Lords, unknown to those about me,
(My fellow Souldiers) first, with what a confidence
I led them on to fight, went on still, and
As if I could have been a second Nature,
As well in heartening them by my example,
As by my exhortation, I gave life
To quicken courage, to inflame revenge,
To heighten resolution; in a word,
To out-doe action: It boots not to discover,
How that young man, who was not fledg'd nor skill'd
In Martial play, was even as ignorant
As childish: But I list not to disparage
His non-ability: The signal given
Of Battel, when our enemies came on,
(Directed more by fury, than by warrant
Of Policy and Stratagem) I met them,
I in the fore-front of the Armies met them;
And as if this old weather-beaten body
Had been compos'd of cannon-proof, I stood
The volleys of their shot. I, I my self
Was he that first dis-rankt their woods of Pikes:
But when we came to handy-stroaks, as often
As I lent blows, so often I gave wounds,
And every wound a death. I may be bold
To justifie a truth, this very sword
Of mine slew more than any twain besides:
And, which is not the least of all my glorie,
When he, this young man, hand to hand in fight,
Was by the General of the Venetians,
And such as were his retinue, unhors'd,
I stept between, and rescu'd him my self,
Or horses hoofs had trampled him to dirt;
And whilst he was re-mounting, I maintain'd
The combate with the gallant General,

Till having taken breath, he throng'd before me,
Renew'd the fight, and with a fatal blow,'
Stole both that honour from me, and his life
From him, whom I before my self alone,
Had more than full three quarters kill'd: a man
Well worthy only by this hand to have dy'd,
Not by a Boys weak push: I talk too much,
But 'tis a fault of age: If to bring home
Long peace, long victorie, even to your Capitol;
If to secure your Kingdom, wives, and children,
Your lives and liberties; if to renown
Your honours through the world, to fix your names,
Like Blazing stars admir'd, and fear'd by all
That have but heard of Candy, or a Cretan,
Be to deserve the approvement of my man-hood,
Then thus much have I done: what more, examine
The annals of my life; and then consider
What I have been, and am. Lords I have said.

GONZALO
With reverence to the Senate, is it lawfull,
Without your Customes breach, to say a word?

POSSENNE
Say on my Lord Gonzalo.

GONZALO
I have heard,
And with no little wonder, such high deeds
Of Chivalrie discours'd, that I confess,
I do not think the Worthies while they liv'd
All nine, deserv'd as much applause, or memorie,
As this one: But who can do ought to gain
The crown of honour from him, must be somewhat
More than a man; you tread a dangerous path,
Yet I shall hear you gladly: for believe me,
Thus much let me profess, in honours cause,
I would not to my Father, nor my King,
(My Countries Father) yield: if you transcend
What we have heard, I can but only say,
That Miracles are yet in use. I fear
I have offended.

PORPHYCIO
You have spoken nobly.
Antinous use your priviledge.

ANTINOUS

Princely Fathers,
E're I begin, one suit I have to make,
'Tis just, and honourable.

POSSENNE
Porphycio
Speak, and have it.

ANTINOUS
That you would please the souldiers might all stand
Together by their General.

POSSENNE
'Tis granted.
All fall to yonder side: Go on, Antinous.

ANTINOUS
I shall be brief and plain: all what my Father
(This Countries Patron) hath discours'd, is true.
Fellows in Arms: speak you, is't true?

SOULDIERS
True, true.

ANTINOUS
It follows, that the blaze of my performance
Took light from what I saw him do: and thus
A City (though the flame be much more dreadfull)
May from a little spark be set on fire;
Of all what I have done, I shall give instance
Only in three main proofs of my desert.
First I sought out (but through how many dangers
My Lords judge ye) the chief, the great Commander,
The head of that huge body, whose proud weight
Our Land shrunk under, him I found and fought with,
Fought with, and slew. Fellows in Arms, speak you,
Is't true or not?

SOULDIERS
True, true.

ANTINOUS
When he was faln,
The hearts of all our adversaries
Began to quail, till young Fernando, son
To the last Duke of Venice gather'd head,
And soon renew'd the field, by whose example
The bold Venetians doubling strength and courage

Had got the better of the day; our men
Supposing that their adversaries grew
Like Hydra's head, recoyle, and 'gan to flye:
I follow'd them; and what I said, they know;
The summe on't is; I call'd them back, new rankt them;
Led on, they follow'd, shrunk not till the end:
Fellows in Arms is't true, or no?

SOULDIERS
True, true.

ANTINOUS
Lastly, to finish all, there was but one,
The only great exploit; which was to take
Fernando prisoner, and that hand to hand
In single fight I did: my self without
The help of any arm, save the arm of Heaven.
Speak Souldiers, is it true, or no?

SOULDIERS
Antinous, Antinous.

ANTINOUS
Behold my prisoner, Fathers.

FERNANDO
This one man
Ruin'd our Army, and hath glorifi'd
Crete in her robes of mightiness and conquest.

POSSENNE
We need not use long circumstance of words,
Antinous thou art conquerer: the Senate,
The souldiers, and thy valour have pronounc'd it.

ALL
Antinous, Antinous.

PORPHYCIO
Make thy demand.

CASSILANES
Please ye (my Lords) give leave
That I may part.

POSSENNE
No Cassilane, the Court
Should therein be dishonour'd, do not imagin

We prize your presence at so slight a rate.
Demand, Antinous.

ANTINOUS
Thus (my Lords) to witness
How far I am from arrogance, or thinking
I am more valiant, though more favour'd
Than my most matchless father, my demand is,
That for a lasting memorie of his name,
His deeds, his real, nay his royal worth,
You set up in your Capitol in Brass
My Fathers Statue, there to stand for ever
A Monument and Trophy of his victories,
With this Inscription to succeeding ages,
Great Cassilanes, Patron of Candy's Peace,
Perpetual Triumpher.

POSSENNE
It is granted. What more?

ANTINOUS
No more.

CASSILANES
How Boy?

GONZALO
Thou art immortal,
Both for thy Son-like pietie, and beauties
Of an unconquer'd minde.

ANTINOUS
My Prisoner, Lords,
To your more sacred wisedoms I surrender:
Fit you his ransom; half whereof I give
For largess to the Souldiers: the other half
To the erection of this monument.

CASSILANES
Ambitious villain.

GONZALO
Thou art all un-imitable.
My Lords, to work a certain peace for Candy
With Venice, use Fernando like a Prince;
His ransom I'le disburse what e're it be:
Yet you may stay him with you, till conditions
Of amitie shall be concluded on:

Are ye content?

PORPHYCIO
We are, and ever rest
Both friends and debters to your nobleness.

GONZALO
Souldiers attend me in the Market-place,
Fie thither send your largess.

SOULDIERS
Antinous, Antinous.

[Exeunt.

CASSILANES
I have a sute too, Lords.

POSSENNE
Propose it, 'tis yours, if fit and just.

CASSILANES
Let not my services,
My being forty years a drudge, a pack-horse
To you, and to the State, be branded now
With Ignominy ne're to be forgotten:
Rear me no Monument, unless you mean
To have me fam'd a Coward, and be stamp'd so.

POSSENNE
We understand you not.

CASSILANES
Proud boy, thou dost,
And Tyrant-like insult'st upon my shame.

ANTINOUS
Sir, Heaven can tell, and my integrity,
What I did, was but only to inforce
The Senates gratitude. I now acknowledge it.

CASSILANES
Observe it Fathers, how this haughty boy
Grows cunning in his envy of mine honours:
He knows no mention can of me be made,
But that it ever likewise must be told,
How I by him was master'd; and for surety
That all succeeding times may so report it,

He would have my dishonour, and his Triumphs
Ingrav'd in Brass: hence, hence proceeds the falshood
Of his insinuating piety.
Thou art no child of mine: thee and thy bloud,
Here in the Capitol, before the Senate,
I utterly renounce: So thrift and fate
Confirm me; henceforth never see my face,
Be, as thou art, a villain to thy Father.
Lords I must crave your leaves: come, come Arcanes.

[Exit.

GONZALO
Here's a strange high-born spirit.

POSSENNE
'Tis but heat
Of suddain present rage; I dare assure Antinous of his favour.

ANTINOUS
I not doubt it,
He is both a good man, and a good Father.
I shall attend your Lordships.

POSSENNE
Do Antinous.

GONZALO
Yes: feast thy Triumphs
With applause and pleasures.

POSSENNE
Lead on.

[Exeunt. Flourish. Cornets.

ANTINOUS
I utterly renounce—'Twas so?
Was't not, my Decius?

DECIUS
Pish, you know, my Lord,
Old men are cholerick.

ANTINOUS
And lastly parted
With, never henceforth see my face: O me,
How have I lost a Father? Such a Father!

Such a one Decius! I am miserable,
Beyond expression.

DECIUS
Fie, how unbecoming
This shews upon your day of fame!

ANTINOUS
O mischief!
I must no more come near him; that I know,
And am assur'd on't.

DECIUS
Say you do not?

ANTINOUS
True:
Put case I do not: what is Candy then
To lost Antinous? Malta, I resolve
To end my dayes in thee.

DECIUS
How's that?

ANTINOUS
I'le trie
All humble means of being reconcil'd,
Which if deny'd, then I may justly say,
This day has prov'd my worst: Decius, my worst.

[Exeunt.

ACTUS SECUNDUS

SCÆNA PRIMA

Enter **GONZALO** and **GASPERO**

GASPERO
Now to what you have heard; as no man can
Better than I, give you her Character;
For I have been both nurs'd, and train'd up to
Her petulant humours, and been glad to bear them,
Her Brother, my late Master, did no less:
Strong apprehensions of her beauty hath
Made her believe that she is more than woman:

And as there did not want those flatterers
'Bout the worlds Conquerour, to make him think,
And did perswade him that he was a god;
So there be those base flies, that will not stick
To buzze into her ears she is an Angel,
And that the food she feeds on is Ambrosia.

GONZALO
She should not touch it then, 'tis Poets fare.

GASPERO
I may take leave to say, she may as well
Determine of her self to be a goddess,
With lesser flatterie than he a god:
For she does conquer more, although not farther.
Every one looks on her, dyes in despair,
And would be glad to do it actually,
To have the next age tell how worthily,
And what good cause he had to perish so:
Here beauty is superlative, she knows it,
And knowing it, thinks no man can deserve,
But ought to perish, and to dye for her:
Many great Princes for her love have languish'd,
And given themselves a willing sacrifice,
Proud to have ended so: And now there is
A Prince so madded in his own passions,
That he forgets the Royaltie he was born to,
And deems it happiness to be her slave.

GONZALO
You talk as if you meant to winde me in,
And make me of the number.

GASPERO
Sir, mistake me not, the service that I owe ye
Shall plead for me: I tell you what she is,
What she expects, and what she will effect,
Unless you be the miracle of men,
That come with a purpose to behold,
And goe away your self.

GONZALO
I thank you, I will do it: But pray resolve me,
How is she stor'd with wit?

GASPERO
As with beauty,
Infinite, and more to be admired at,

Than medled with.

GONZALO
And walks her tongue the same gate with her feet?

GASPERO
Much beyond: what e're her heart thinks, she utters:
And so boldly, so readily, as you would judge
It penn'd and studied.

[Enter **EROTO, PHILANDER, ANNOPHIL, HYPARCHA, MOCHINGO** & **ATTENDANTS**

GONZALO
She comes.

GASPERO
I must leave you then,
But my best wishes shall remain with you.

[Exit.

GONZALO
Still I must thank you.
This is the most passionate,
Most pitifull Prince,
Who in the Caldron of affections,
Looks as he had been par-boy'ld.

PHILANDER
If I offend with too much loving you,
It is a fault that I must still commit,
To make your mercy shine the more on me.

EROTA
You are the self-same creature you condemn,
Or else you durst not follow me with hope
That I can pity you, who am so far
From granting any comfort in this kind,
That you and all men else shall perish first:
I will live free and single, till I find
Something above a man to equal me;
Put all your brave Heroes into one,
Your Kings and Emperours, and let him come
In person of a man, and I should scorn him:
Must, and will scorn him.
The god of love himself hath lost his eyes,
His Bow and Torch extinguish'd, and the Poets
That made him first a god, have lost their fire

Since I appear'd, and from my eyes must steal it.
This I dare speak; and let me see the man,
Now I have spoke it, that doth, dare deny;
Nay, not believe it.

MOCHINGO
He is mad that does not.

EROTA
Have not all the nations of the Earth heard of me?
Most come to see me, and seeing me, return'd
Full of my praises? teaching their Chroniclers
To make their Stories perfect? for where the name,
Merely the word of fair Erota stands,
It is a lasting History to time,
Begetting admiration in the men,
And in my own Sex envie: which glorie's lost,
When I shall stick my beautie in a cloud,
And clearly shine through it.

GONZALO
This woman's in the altitudes, and he must be
A good Astrologer shall know her Zodiack.

PHILANDER
For any man to think
Himself an able purchaser of you,
But in the bargain there must be declar'd
Infinite bounty: otherwise I vow,
By all that's excellent and gracious in you,
I would untenant every hope lodg'd in me,
And yield my self up loves, or your own Martyr.

EROTA
So you shall please us.

PHILANDER
O you cannot be
So heavenly, and so absolute in all things,
And yet retain such cruel tyranny.

EROTA
I can, I do, I will.

GONZALO
She is in her
Moods, and her Tenses: I'le Grammer with you,
And make a trial how I can decline you:

By your leave (great Lady.)

EROTA
What are you?

GONZALO
A man, a good man, that's a wealthy;
A Proper man, and a proud man too; one
That understands himself, and knows, unless
It be your self, no woman on the Universe deserves him.
Nay, Lady, I must tell you too withal,
I may make doubt of that, unless you paint
With better judgement next day than on this;
For (plain I must be with you) 'tis a dull Fucus.

EROTA
Knows any one here what this fellow is?

ATTENDANTS
He is of Venice (Madam) a great Magnifico,
And gracious with the Senate.

EROTA
Let him keep then among them; what makes he here?
Here's state enough where I am: here's a do—
You, tell him, if he have ought with us, let him
Look lower, and give it in Petition.

MOCHINGO
Mighty Magnifico, my Mistris bid me tell you,
If you have ought with her, you must look lower,
And yield it in Petition.

GONZALO
Here is for thee a Ducket.

MOCHINGO
You say well Sir, take your own course.

GONZALO
I will not grace you
(Lady) so much as take you by the hand;
But when I shall vouchsafe to touch your lip,
It shall be through your Court a holy-day
Proclaimed for so high favour.

EROTA
This is some

Great mans Jester: Sirrah, begon, here is
No place to fool in.

GONZALO
Where are the fools you talk of?
I do keep two.

EROTA
No question of it: for
In your self you do maintain an hundred.

GONZALO
And besides them I keep a noble train,
Statists, and men of aclion: my purse is large and deep,
Beyond the reach of riot to draw drie:
Fortune did vie with Nature, to bestow
(When I was born) her bountie equally:
'Tis not amiss you turn your eyes from me;
For should you stand and gaze me in the face,
You perish would, like Semele by Jove:
In Venice at this instant there do lye
No less than threescore Ladies in their graves,
And in their Beds five hundred for my love.

MOCHINGO
You lie more than they; yet it becomes him bravely;
Would I could walk and talk so! I'le endeavour it.

EROTA
Sir, do you know me?

GONZALO
Yes, you were sister to the late Prince of Candy,
Aunt to this young one: and I in Venice,
Am born a Lord; equall to you in fortunes,
In shape; I'le say no more, but view.

MOCHINGO
There needs no more be said, were I a woman—
O he does rarely: in shape; I'le say no more,
But view: who could say more, who better?
Man is no man, nor woman woman is,
Unless they have a pride like one of these.
How poor the Prince of Cyprus shews to him!
How poor another Lady unto her!
Carriage and State makes us seem demi-gods,
Humility, like beasts, worms of the Earth.

[Enter **ANTINOUS**, and **DECIUS**.

ANTINOUS
Royal Lady, I kiss your hand.

EROTA
Sir, I know you not.

ANNOPHEL
O my noble Brother, welcom from the wars.

ANTINOUS
Dear Sister.

ANNOPHEL
Where is my Father, that you come without him?
We have news of your success: he has his health I hope?

ANTINOUS
Yes Sister, he has his health, but is not well.

ANNOPHEL
How not well? what Riddles do you utter?

ANTINOUS
I'le tell you more in private.

GONZALO
Noble Sir,
I cannot be unmindfull of your merit,
Since I last heard it: you are a hopefull youth,
And (indeed) the Soul of Candy.
I must speak my thoughts.

ANNOPHEL
The Prince of Cyprus Brother, good Decius.

ANTINOUS
I am his Servant.

PHILANDER
You are the Patron of your Countrie, Sir,
So your unimitable deeds proclaim you,
It is no language of my own, but all mens.

GONZALO
Your Enemies must needs acknowledge it:
Then do not think it flatterie in your friends,

For if they had a heart, they could not want a tongue.

EROTA
Is this your Brother Annophil?

ANNOPHEL
Yes Madam.

EROTA
Your name's Antinous?

ANTINOUS
I am (Lady) that most unfortunate man.

EROTA
How unfortunate? are you not the Souldier,
The Captain of those Captains, that did bring
Conquest and Victory home along with you?

ANTINOUS
I had some share in't; but was the least
Of the least worthy.

GONZALO
O Sir, in your modesty you'ld make
A double Conquest: I was an ear-witness
When this young man spoke lesser than he acted,
And had the Souldiers voice to help him out:
But that the Law compell'd him for his honour,
To inforce him make a claim for his reward,
I well perceive he would have stood the man
That he does now, buried his worth in silence.

EROTA
Sir, I hearken not to him, but look on you,
And find more in you than he can relate:
You shall attend on me.

ANTINOUS
Madam, your pardon.

EROTA
Deny it not Sir, for it is more honour
Than you have gotten i'th' field: for know you shall,
Upon Erota's asking, serve Erota.

ANTINOUS
I may want answers, Lady,

But never want a will to do you service.
I came here to my Sister, to take leave,
Having enjoyn'd my self to banishment,
For some cause that hereafter you may hear,
And wish with me I had not the occasion.

ANNOPHEL
There shall be no occasion to divide us:
Dear Madam for my sake use your power,
Even for the service that he ought to owe,
Must, and does owe to you, his friends, and country.

EROTA
Upon your Loyalty to the state and me,
I do command you Sir, not depart Candy:
Am I not your Princess?

ANTINOUS
You are a great Lady.

EROTA
Then shew your self a Servant and a Subject.

ANTINOUS
I am your vassal.

MOCHINGO
You are a Coward; I that dare not fight,
Scorn to be vassail to any Prince in Europe:
Great is my heart with pride, which I'le encrease
When they are gone, with practise on my Vassals.

ATTENDANTS
The noble Cassilane is come to see you Madam.

ANTINOUS
For here's the place, and persons that have power,
To reconcile you to his love again.

DECIUS
There's comfort in those words, Antinous
For here's the place, and persons that have power,
To reconcile you to his love again.

ANTINOUS
That were a fortunate meeting.

[Enter **CASSILANES** and **ARCANES**.

CASSILANES
Greatness still wait you Lady.

EROTA
Good Cassilane, we do maintain our greatness,
Through your valour.

CASSILANES
My prayers pull daily blessings on thy head,
My un-offending child, my Annophel.
Good Prince, worthy Gonzalo! ha? art thou here
Before me? in every action art thou ambitious?
My duty (Lady) first offered here,
And love to thee (my child) though he out-strip me;
Thus in the wars he got the start on me,
By being forward, but performing less;
All the endeavours of my life are lost,
And thrown upon that evil of mine own
Cursed begetting, whom I shame to father.
O that the heat thou rob'dst me of, had burnt
Within my Entrails, and begot a feaver,
Or some worse sickness, for thou art a disease
Sharper than any Physick gives a name to.

ANNOPHEL
Why do you say so?

CASSILANES
O Annophil; there is good cause my girle:
He has plaid the thief with me, and filch'd away
The richest jewel of my life, my honour,
Wearing it publickly with that applause,
As if he justly did inherit it.

ANTINOUS
Would I had in my Infancy been laid
Within my grave, covered with your blessings rather
Than grown up to a man, to meet your curses.

CASSILANES
O that thou hadst.
Then I had been the Father of a child,
Dearer than thou wert ever unto me,
When hope perswaded me I had begot
Another self in thee: Out of mine eyes,
As far as I have thrown thee from my heart,
That I may live and dye forgetting thee.

EROTA

How has he deserv'd this untam'd anger,
That when he might have ask't for his reward
Some honour for himself, or mass of pelf,
He only did request to have erected
Your Statue in the Capitol, with Titles
Ingrav'd upon't, The Patron of his Countrey?

CASSILANES

That, that's the poison in the gilded cup,
The Serpent in the flowers, that stings my honour,
And leaves me dead in fame: Gods do a justice,
And rip his bosom up, that men may see,
Seeing, believe the subtle practises
Written within his heart: But I am heated,
And do forget this presence, and my self.
Your pardon, Lady.

EROTA

You should not ask, 'less you knew how to give.
For my sake Cassilane, cast out of your thoughts
All ill conceptions of your worthy son,
That (questionless) has ignorantly offended,
Declared in his penitence.

CASSILANES

Bid me dye, Lady, for your sake I'le do it;
But that you'l say is nothing, for a man
That has out-liv'd his honour: But command me
In any thing save that, and Cassilane
Shall ever be your servant. Come Annophel,
(My joy in this world) thou shalt live with me,
(Retired in some solitarie nook,)
The comfort of my age; my dayes are short,
And ought to be well spent: and I desire
No other witness of them but thy self,
And good Arcanes.

ANNOPHEL

I shall obey you Sir.

GONZALO

Noble Sir:
If you taste any want of worldly means,
Let not that discontent you: know me your friend,
That hath, and can supply you.

CASSILANES
Sir, I am too much bound to you already,
And 'tis not of my cares the least, to give you
Fair satisfaction.

GONZALO
You may imagine I do speak to that end,
But trust me, 'tis to make you bolder with me.

CASSILANES
Sir, I thank you, and may make trial of you,
Mean time my service.

ANNOPHEL
Brother be comforted; so long as I continue
Within my Fathers love, you cannot long
Stand out an Exile: I must goe live with him,
And I will prove so good an Orator
In your behalf, that you again shall gain him,
Or I will stir in him another anger,
And be lost with you.

ANTINOUS
Better I were neglected: for he is hasty,
And through the Choler that abounds in him,
(Which for the time divides from him his judgement)
He may cast you off, and with you his life;
For grief will straight surprize him, and that way
Must be his death: the sword has try'd too often,
And all the deadly Instruments of war
Have aim'd at his great heart, but ne're could touch it:
Yet not a limb about him wants a scar.

CASSILANES
Madam my duty—

EROTA
Will you be gone?

CASSILANES
I must, Lady, but I shall be ready,
When you are pleas'd command me, for your service.
Excellent Prince—To all my heartie love,
And a good Farewel.

MOCHINGO
Thanks honest Cassilane.

CASSILANES
Come Annophel.

GONZALO
Shall I not wait upon you Sir?

CASSILANES
From hence you shall not stir a foot:
Loving Gonzalo, it must be all my study
To requite you.

GONZALO
If I may be so fortunate to deserve
The name of friend from you, I have enough.

CASSILANES
You are so, and you have made your self so.

GONZALO
I will then preserve it.

EROTA
Antinous you are my servant, are you not?

ANTINOUS
It hath pleased you so to grace me.

EROTA
Why are you then dejected? you will say,
You have lost a father; but you have found a Mistris
Doubles that loss: be master of your spirit;
You have a cause for it, which is my favour.

GONZALO
And mine.

EROTA
Will no man ease me of this fool?

GONZALO
Your fellow.

EROTA
Antinous wait upon us.

ANTINOUS
I shall Madam.

GONZALO
Nay but Ladie, Ladie.

EROTA
Sir, you are rude: and if you be the Master
Of such means as you do talk of, you should
Learn good manners.

GONZALO
O Lady, you can find a fault in me,
But not perceive it in your self: you must, shall hear me:
I love you for your pride, 'tis the best vertue
In you.

EROTA
I could hang this fellow now: by whom
Are you supported, that you dare do this?
Have you not example here in a Prince
Transcending you in all things, yet bears himself
As doth become a man had seen my beautie?
Back to your Country, and your Curtizans,
Where you may be admired for your wealth,
Which being consum'd, may be a means to gain you
The opinion of some wit. Here's nothing
To be got but scorn, and loss of time.

GONZALO
Which are things I delight in.

EROTA
Antinous follow me.

[Exit.

GONZALO
She is vext to the soul.

MOCHINGO
Let her be vext, 'tis fit she should be so:
Give me thy hand Gonzalo, thou art in our favour,
For we do love to cherish lofty spirits,
Such as percusse the Earth, and bound
With an erected countenance to the clouds.

GONZALO
'S-foot, what thing is this?

MOCHINGO

I do love fire-works, because they mount:
An Exhalation I profess to adore,
Beyond a fixed star, 'tis more illustrious,
As every thing rais'd out of smoak is so:
Their vertue is in action: what do you think of me?

GONZALO
Troth Sir,
You are beyond my ghess, I know you not.

MOCHINGO
Do you know your self?

GONZALO
Yes Sir.

MOCHINGO
Why you and I are one: I am proud, and
Very proud too, that I must tell you; I saw
It did become you, cousin Gonzalo, prethee
Let it be so.

GONZALO
Let it be so good cousin.

MOCHINGO
I am no great ones fool.

GONZALO
I hope so, for alliance sake.

MOCHINGO
Yet I do serve the Mighty, Monstrous, and Magnanimous
Invincible Erota.

GONZALO
O good cousin, now I have you: I'le meet you in your Coat.

MOCHINGO
Coat? I have my horse-mans coat I must confess
Lin'd through with Velvet, and a Scarlet out-side;
If you'll meet me in't, I'le send for't;
And cousin you shall see me with much comfort,
For it is both a new one, and a right one,
It did not come collateral.

GONZALO
Adieu good cousin; at this present I have some business.

MOCHINGO
Farewel, excellent cousin.

Enter **GONZALO** and **FERNANDO**.

GONZALO
Candy, I say, is lost already.

FERNANDO
Yes,
If to be conqueror be to be lost.

GONZALO
You have it; one days conquest hath undone them.
And sold them to their vassalage; for what
Have I else toyl'd my brains, profusely emptied
My moneys, but to make them slaves to Venice,
That so in case the sword did lose his edge,
Then art might sharpen hers?

FERNANDO
Gonzalo how?

GONZALO
Fernando thus: you see how through this Land,
Both of the best and basest I am honour'd;
I only gave the State of Venice notice,
When, where, and how to land, or you had found
A better entertainment: I was he
Encourag'd young Antinous to affront
The Devil his Father: for the Devil I think
Dares not do more in battel.

FERNANDO
But why did ye?
I find no such great policie in that.

GONZALO
Indeed Fernando, thou canst fight, not plot:
Had they continu'd one, they two alone
Were of sufficient courage and performance

To beat an Armie.

FERNANDO
Now by all my hopes,
I rather shall admire, than envy vertue.

GONZALO
Why then by all your hopes you'l rather have
Your Brains knockt out, than learn how to be wise;
You States-man? Well Sir, I did more than this,
When Cassilane crav'd from the common treasure
Pay for his Souldiers, I strook home, and lent him
An hundred thousand Duckets.

FERNANDO
Marry Sir,
The policy was little, the love less,
And honesty least of all.

GONZALO
How say ye by that?
Go fight, I say goe fight, I'le talk no more with you,
You are insensible.

FERNANDO
Well, I shall observe ye.

GONZALO
Why look you Sir, by this means have I got
The greatest part of Cassilanes estate
Into my hands, which he can ne're redeem,
But must of force sink: do you conceive me now?

FERNANDO
So:
But why have you importuned the Senate,
For me to sojourn with them?

GONZALO
There's the quintessence,
The soul, and grand elixir of my wit:
For he (according to his noble nature)
Will not be known to want, though he do want,
And will be bankrupted so much the sooner,
And made the subject of our scorn and laughter.

FERNANDO
Here's a perfect plotted stratagem.

GONZALO
Why? could you
Imagine, that I did not hate in heart
My Countryes enemies? yes, yes, Fernando,
And I will be the man that shall undoe them.

FERNANDO
Ye are in a ready way.

GONZALO
I was never out on't.

[Enter **GASPERO**.

GONZALO
Peace,
Here comes a wise Coxcombe, a tame Coward.
Now worthy Gaspero, what,
You come (I know) to be my Lord Fernando's
Conducter to old Cassilane?

GASPERO
To wait upon him.

GONZALO
And my Lords the Senators sent you?

GASPERO
My noble Lord they did.

GONZALO
My Lord Fernando,
This Gentleman, (as humble as you see him)
Is even this Kingdoms treasure; In a word,
'Tis his chief glory that he is not wiser
Than honest, nor more honest than approv'd
In truth and faith.

GASPERO
My Lord.

GONZALO
You may be bold
To trust him with your bosom, he'l not deceive
If you relie upon him once.

FERNANDO

Your name is Gaspero?

GASPERO
Your servant.

GONZALO
Go commend me
(Right honest Gaspero) commend me heartily
To noble Cassilane, tell him my love
Is vow'd to him.

GASPERO
I shall.

GONZALO
I know you will.
My Lord I cannot long be absent from you.

FERNANDO
Sir, you are now my guide.

[Exit.

GONZALO
Thus my designs
Run uncontroul'd; yet Venice though I be
Intelligencer to thee, in my brain
Are other large Projects: for if proud Erota
Bend to my lure, I will be Candy's King,
And Duke of Venice too. Ha? Venice too?
O 'twas prettily shov'd in: why not? Erota
May in her love seal all sure: if she swallow
The bait, I am Lord of both; if not, yet Candy
Despight of all her power shall be ruin'd.

[Enter **CASSILANES**, **ARCANES**, and **ANNOPHEL**

CASSILANES
Urge me no farther Annopbel.

ANNOPHEL
My Lord.

CASSILANES
Thy fathers poverty has made thee happy;
For though 'tis true, this solitary life
Sutes not with youth and beautie, O my child,
Yet 'tis the sweetest Guardian to protect

Chast names from Court aspersions; there a Lady
Tender and delicate in years and graces,
That doats upon the charms of ease and pleasure,
Is ship-wrackt on the shore; for 'tis much safer
To trust the Ocean in a leaking ship,
Than follow greatness in the wanton rites
Of luxurie and sloth.

ANNOPHEL
My wishes Sir,
Have never soar'd a higher flight, than truly
To find occasion wherein I might witness
My duty and obedience.

CASSILANES
'Tis well said,
Canst thou forbear to laugh Arcanes?

ARCANES
Why Sir?

CASSILANES
To look upon my beggerie, to look upon
My patience in my beggerie: Tell me,
Does it shew handsom? bravely?
Handsom? thou wilt flatter me,
And swear that I am miserable.

ARCANES
Nothing
More glorifies the noble, and the valiant,
Than to despise contempt: if you continue
But to enjoy your self, you in your self
Enjoy all store besides.

CASSILANES
An excellent change:
I that some seven Apprentice-ships commanded
A hundred Ministers, that waited on
My nod, and sometimes twenty thousand souldiers,
Am now retir'd, attended in my age
By one poor maid, follow'd by one old man.

ARCANES
Sir, you are lower in your own repute
Than you have reason for.

CASSILANES

The Roman Captains,
I mean the best, such as with their blouds
Purchas'd their Countreys peace, the Empires glorie,
Were glad at last to get them to some Farmes,
Off-from the clamours of the ingratefull great ones,
And the unsteady multitude, to live
As I do now, and 'twas their blessing too,
Let it be ours Arcanes.

ARCANES
I cannot but
Applaud your scorn of injuries.

CASSILANES
Of injuries?
Arcanes, Annophel, lend both your hands.
So, what say ye now?

ARCANES
Why now my Lord—

CASSILANES
I swear
By all my past prosperities; thus standing
Between you two, I think my self as great,
As mighty, as if in the Capitol
I stood amidst the Senators, with all
The Cretan subjects prostrate at my feet.

ANNOPHEL
Sir, you are here more safe.

CASSILANES
And more beloved:
Why look ye Sirs, I can forget the weakness
Of the traduced Souldiers, the negleft
Of the fair-spoken Senate, the impietie
Of him, the villain, whom (to my dishonour)
The World miscalls my son.
But by the—

ARCANES
Sir, remember that you promis'd no occasion
Should move your patience.

CASSILANES
Thou do'st chide me friendly,
He shall not have the honour to be thought upon

Amongst us.

[Enter a **SERVANT**.

Now? the news?

SERVANT
The Secretarie,
With the Venetian prisoner, desire
Admittance to your Lordship.

CASSILANES
How? to me?
What mysterie is this? Arcanes can they,
Thinkst thou, mean any good?

ARCANES
My Lord, they dare not
Intend ought else but good.

CASSILANES
'Tis true, they dare not;
Arcanes welcom them: Come hither Annophel,
Stand close to me, we'l change our affability
Into a form of State: and they shall know
Our heart is still our own.

[Enter **ARCANES**, **FERNANDO**, and **GASPERO**.

ARCANES
My Lord—

CASSILANES
Arcanes,
I know them both: Fernando, as you are
A man of greatness, I should under-value
The right my sword hath fought for, to observe
Low-fawning complements, but as you are
A Captive and a stranger, I can love you,
And must be kind. You are welcom.

FERNANDO
'Tis the all
Of my ambition.

GASPERO
And for proof how much
He truly honours your heroick vertues,

The Senate on his importunity,
Commend him to your Lordships guard.

CASSILANES
For what?

GASPERO
During the time of his abode in Candy,
To be your houshold guest.

FERNANDO
Wherein my Lord,
You shall more make me debtor to your nobleness,
Than if you had return'd me without ransom.

CASSILANES
Are you in earnest Sir?

FERNANDO
My sute to the Senate
Shall best resolve you that.

CASSILANES
Come hither Secretarie,
Look that this be no trick now put upon me:
For if it be—Sirrah—

GASPERO
As I have troth
(My Lord) it only is a favour granted
Upon Fernando's motion, from himself:
Your Lordship must conceive, I'de not partake
Ought, but what should concern your honour; Who
Has been the prop, our Countries shield, and safety,
But the renowned Cassilane?

CASSILANES
Applause?
Is Gaspero—puff—nothing—why, young Lord,
Would you so much be sequester'd from those
That are the blazing Comets of the time,
To live a solitary life with me?
A man forsaken? all my hospitality
Is now contracted to a few; these two,
The tempest-wearied Souldier, and this Virgin;
We cannot feast your eyes with Masques and Revels,
Or Courtly Anticks; the sad Sports we riot in,
Are tales of foughten fields, of Martial scars,

And things done long ago, when men of courage
Were held the best, not those well-spoken Youths,
Who only carry Conquest in their tongues:
Now stories of this nature are unseasonable
To entertain a great Duke's Son with.

FERNANDO
Herein
Shall my Captivity be made my happiness,
Since what I lose in freedom, I regain
(With int'rest) by conversing with a Souldier,
So matchless for experience, as great Cassilane:
'Pray Sir, admit me.

CASSILANES
If you, come to mock me,
I shall be angry.

FERNANDO
By the love I bear
To goodness, my intents are honourable.

CASSILANES
Then in a word, my Lord, your visitations
Shall find all due respect: but I am now
Grown old, and have forgot to be an Host;
Come when you please, you are welcome.

FERNANDO
Sir, I thank you.

ANNOPHEL
Good Sir, be not too urgent; for my Father
Will soon be mov'd: yet, in a noble way
Of courtesie, he is as easily conquer'd.

FERNANDO
Lady, your words are like your beauty, powerful;
I shall not strive more how to do him service
Than how to be your servant.

CASSILANES
She's my Daughter,
And does command this House.

FERNANDO
So I conceive her.

CASSILANES
Do you hear?

GASPERO
My honour'd Lord.

CASSILANES
Commend me to them:
Tell 'em I thank them.

GASPERO
Whom, my Lord?

CASSILANES
The Senate;
Why, how come you so dull? O they are gracious,
And infinitely grateful—Thou art eloquent,
Speak modestly in mentioning my services;
And if ought fall out in the By, that must
Of meer necessity touch any act
Of my deserving praises, blush when you talk on't,
Twill make them blush to hear on't.

GASPERO
Why, my Lord—

CASSILANES
Nay, nay, you are too wise now; good, observe me.
I do not rail against the hopeful Springall,
That builds up Monuments in Brass; rears Trophies
With Mottoes and Inscriptions, quaint devices
Of Poetry and Fiction; let's be quiet.

ARCANES
You must not cross him.

GASPERO
Not for Candy's Wealth.

FERNANDO
You shall for ever make me yours.

ANNOPHEL
'Twere pity to double your Captivity.

ARCANES
Who's here, Decius?

[Enter **DECIUS**.

CASSILANES
Ha! Decius? who nam'd Decius?

DECIUS
My duty to your Lordship, I am bold,
Presuming on your noble, and known goodness
To—

CASSILANES
What?

DECIUS
Present you with this—

CASSILANES
Letter?

DECIUS
Yes, my honour'd Lord.

CASSILANES
From whom?

DECIUS
'Please you peruse
The inside, and you shall find a name subscrib'd,
In such humility, in such obedience,
That you your self will judge it tyranny
Not to receive it favourably.

CASSILANES
Hey-day!
Good words my Masters: this is Court-infection,
And none but Cowards ply them: tell me, Decius,
Without more circumstance, who is the Sender?

DECIUS
Your most griev'd Son, Antinous.

CASSILANES
On my life
A Challenge; speak, as thou art worthy, speak;
I'll answer't.

DECIUS
Honour'd Sir.

CASSILANES
No honour'd Sirs—
Fool your young Idol with such pompous Attributes.
Say briefly, what contains it?

DECIUS
'Tis a lowly
Petition for your favour.

CASSILANES
Rash young man,
But that thou art under my own roof, and know'st
I dare not any way infringe the Laws
Of Hospitality, thou should'st repent
Thy bold and rude intrusion. But presume not
Again to shew thy Letter, for thy life;
Decius, not for thy life.

ARCANES
Nay then, (my Lord)
I can with-hold no longer; you are too rough,
And wrestle against nature with a violence
More than becomes a Father; wherein would ye
Come nearer to the likeness of God,
Than in your being entreated? Let not thirst
Of Honour, make you quite forget you are
A Man, and what makes perfect manhoods, comforts
A Father.

ANNOPHEL
If a memory remain
Of my departed Mother; if the purity
Of her unblemish'd faith deserve to live
In your remembrance, let me yet by these
Awake your love to my uncomforted Brother.

FERNANDO
I am a Stranger, but so much I tender
Your Sons desertful Vertues, that I vow
His Sword ne'r conquer'd me so absolutely,
As shall your courtesie, if you vouchsafe
At all our instances, to new receive him
Into your wonted favour.

GASPERO
Sir, you cannot
Require more low submission.

ANNOPHEL
Am I not
Grown vile yet in your eyes? then by the name
Of Father, let me once more sue for him,
Who is the only now remaining Branch
With me, of that most ancient root, whose Body
You are, dear Sir.

CASSILANES
'Tis well, an host of furies
Could not have baited me more torturingly,
More rudely, or more most unnaturally.
Decius, I say, let me no more hear from him;
For this time go thou hence, and know from me
Thou art beholding to me that I have not
Kill'd thee already, look to't next, look to't.
Arcanes fie, fie Annophel.

[Exit.

ARCANES
He's gone;
Chaf'd beyond sufferance; we must follow him.

DECIUS
Lady, this Letter is to you.

ANNOPHEL
Come with me,
For we must speak in private; 'please you, Sir,
To see what entertainment our sad house
Can yield?

[Exit.

FERNANDO
I shall attend you, Lady.

GASPERO
How do you like
To sojourn here, my Lord?

FERNANDO
More than to feast
With all the Princes of the Earth besides:
Gonzalo told me that thou wert honest.

GASPERO
Yes Sir,
And you shall find it.

FERNANDO
Shall I?

GASPERO
All my follies
Be else recorded to my shame.

FERNANDO
Enough,
My heart is here for ever lodg'd.

GASPERO
The Lady.

FERNANDO
The place admits no time to utter all,
But Gaspero if thou wilt prove my friend,
I'll say thou art—

GASPERO
Your Servant; I conceive ye,
We'll chuse some fitter leisure.

FERNANDO
Never man
Was (in a moment) or more bless'd or wretched.

[Exeunt.

[Enter **HYPARCHA**, placing two Chairs, **ANTINOUS** and **EROTA**.

EROTA
Leave us.

HYPARCHA
I shall.

[Exit.

EROTA
Antinous, sit down.

ANTINOUS
Madam.

EROTA

I say sit down, I do command you sit;
For look what honour thou dost gain by me,
I cannot lose it: happy Antinous,
The graces and the higher Deities
Smil'd at thy Birth, and still continue it:
Then think that I (who scorn lesser examples)
Must do the like: such as do taste my power,
And talk of it with fear and reverence,
Shall do the same unto the man I favour.
I tell thee Youth, thou hast a conquest won,
Since thou cam'st home, greater than that last,
Which dignified thy Fame, greater than if
Thou should'st go out again, and conquer farther;
For I am not ashamed to acknowledge
My self subdued by thee.

ANTINOUS

Great Lady—

EROTA

Sit still, I will not hear thee else; now speak,
And speak like my Antinous, like my Souldier,
Whom Cupid, and not Mars hath sent to Battel.

ANTINOUS

I must (I see) be silent.

EROTA

So thou maist;
There's greater action in it than in clamour,
A look (if it be gracious) will begin the War,
A word conclude it; then prove no Coward,
Since thou hast such a friendly enemy,
That teaches thee to conquer.

ANTINOUS

You do amaze me, Madam,
I have no skill, no practice in this War,
And whether you be serious, or please
To make your sport on a dejected man,
I cannot rightly guess; but be it as it will,
It is a like unhappiness to me:
My discontents bear those conditions in them,
And lay me out so wretched, no designs
(However truly promising a good)
Can make me relish ought but a sweet-bitter

Voluntary Exile.

EROTA
Why an Exile?
What comfort can there be in those Companions
Which sad thoughts bring along with?

[Enter **HYPARCHA**

HYPARCHA
Madam.

MUSICK.

EROTA
Whence comes this well tun'd sound?

HYPARCHA
I know not, Madam.

EROTA
Listen Wench;
What ever friendly hands they are that send it,

SONG

Let 'em play on; they are Masters of their faculty:
Doth it please you, Sir?

ANTINOUS
According to the time.

EROTA
Go to 'em, Wench,
And tell 'em, we shall thank 'em; for they have kept
As good time to our disposition, as to their instruments;
Unless Antinous shall say he loves,
There never can be sweeter accents utter'd.

[Enter **PHILANDER**.

PHILANDER
Let then the heart that did employ those hands,
Receive some small share of your thanks with them,
'Tis happiness enough that you did like it;
A fortune unto me, that I should send it
In such a lucky minute; but to obtain
So gracious welcome did exceed my hopes.

EROTA

Good Prince, I thank you for't.

PHILANDER

O Madam, pour not (too fast) joys on me,
But sprinkle 'em so gently I may stand 'em;
It is enough at first, you have laid aside
Those cruel angry looks out of your eyes,
With which (as with your lovely) you did strike
All your Beholders in an Ecstasie.

EROTA

Philander, you have long profest to love me.

PHILANDER

Have I but profest it, Madam?

EROTA

Nay, but hear me?

PHILANDER

More attentively than to an Oracle.

EROTA

And I will speak more truly, if more can be;
Nor shall my language be wrapt up in Riddles,
But plain as truth it self; I love this Gentleman,
Whose grief has made him so uncapable
Of Love, he will not hear, at least not understand it.
I, that have lookt with scornful eyes on thee,
And other Princes, mighty in their states,
And in their friends as fortunate, have now pray'd,
In a petitionary kind almost,
This man, this well-deserving man, (that I must say)
To look upon this beauty, yet you see
He casts his eyes rather upon the ground,
Than he will turn 'em this way; Philander,
You look pale; I'll talk no more.

PHILANDER

Pray go forward; I would be your Martyr,
To dye thus, were immortally to live.

EROTA

Will you go to him then, and speak for me?
You have loved longer, but not ferventer,
Know how to speak, for you have done it like

An Orator, even for your self; then how will you for me
Whom you profess to love above your self.

PHILANDER
The Curses of Dissemblers follow me
Unto my Grave, and if I do not so.

EROTA
You may (as all men do) speak boldlier, better
In their friends cause still, than in your own;
But speak your utmost, yet you cannot feign,
I will stand by, and blush to witness it.
Tell him, since I beheld him, I have lost
The happiness of this life, food, and rest;
A quiet bosome, and the state I went with.
Tell him how he has humbled the proud,
And made the living but a dead Erota.
Tell him withal, that she is better pleas'd
With thinking on him, than enjoying these.
Tell him—Philander, Prince; I talk in vain
To you, you do not mark me.

PHILANDER
Indeed I do.

EROTA
But thou dost look so pale,
As thou wilt spoil the story in relating.

PHILANDER
Not, if I can but live to tell it.

EROTA
It may be you have not the heart.

PHILANDER
I have a will I am sure how e'r my heart
May play the Coward, but if you please, I'll try.

EROTA
If a kiss will strengthen thee, I give you leave
To challenge it, nay, I will give it you.

PHILANDER
O that a man should taste such heavenly bliss,
And be enjoyn'd to beg it for another!

EROTA

Alas, it is a misery I grieve
To put you to, and I will suffer rather
In his tyranny, than thou in mine.

PHILANDER
Nay Madam, since I cannot have your love,
I will endeavour to deserve your pity;
For I had rather have within the grave
Your love, than you should want it upon earth.
But how can I hope, with a feeble tongue
To instruct him in the rudiments of love,
When your most powerful Beauty cannot work it?

EROTA
Do what thou wilt (Philander) the request
Is so unreasonable, that I quit thee of it.
I desire now no more but the true patience,
And fortitude of Lovers, with those helps
Of sighs and tears, which I think is all the Physick—

PHILANDER
O if he did but hear you 'twere enough;
And I will 'wake him from his Apoplexie.
Antinous.

ANTINOUS
My Lord?

PHILANDER
Nay, 'pray,
No courtesie to me, you are my Lord,
(Indeed you are) for you command her heart
That commands mine; nor can you want to know it.
For look you, she that told it you in words,
Explains it now more passionately in tears;
Either thou hast no heart, or a marble one,
If those drops cannot melt it; prithee look up
And see how sorrow sits within her eyes,
And love the grief she goes with (if not her)
Of which thou art the Parent; and never yet
Was there (by Nature) that thing made so stony
But it would love what ever it begot.

ANTINOUS
He that begot me did beget these cares
Which are good issues, though happily by him
Esteemed Monsters: Nay, the ill-judging World
Is likely enough to give them those Characters.

PHILANDER
What's this to love, and to the Lady? he's old,
Wrathful, perverse, self-will'd, and full of anger,
Which are his faults; but let them not be thine;
He thrusts you from his love, she pulls thee on;
He doubts your Vertues, she doth double them;
O either use thine own eyes, or take mine,
And with them my heart, then thou wilt love her,
Nay, dote upon her more than on thy duty,
And men will praise thee equally for it,
Neglecting her, condemn thee as a man
Unworthy such a fortune: O Antinous,
'Tis not the friendship that I bear to thee,
But her command, that makes me utter this;
And when I have prevail'd, let her but say,
Philander, you must dye or this is nothing,
It shall be done together with a breath,
With the same willingness I live to serve her.

EROTA
No more, Philander.

PHILANDER
All I have done, is little yet to purpose,
But ere I leave him I will perceive him blush;
And make him feel the passions that I do,
And every true Lover will assist me in't,
And lend me their sad sighs to blow it home,
For Cupid wants a Dart to wound this bosome.

EROTA
No more, no more, Philander, I can endure no more,
Pray let him go; go good Antinous, make peace
With your own mind, no matter though I perish.

[Exit.

ACTUS QUARTUS

SCÆNA PRIMA

Enter **HYPARCHA**, and **MOCHINGO**

HYPARCHA
I Cannot help it.

MOCHINGO
Nor do I require it,
The malady needs no Physician,
Help hospital people.

HYPARCHA
I am glad to hear
You are so valiant.

MOCHINGO
Valiant?
Can any man be proud that is not valiant?
Foolish Woman, what would'st thou say? thou—
know not what to call thee.

HYPARCHA
I can you,
For I can call you Coxcomb, Ass, and Puppy.

MOCHINGO
You do doe it, I thank you.

HYPARCHA
That you'll lose a Fortune,
Which a Cobler better deserves than thou dost.

MOCHINGO
Do not provoke my magnanimity,
For when I am incens'd I am insensible,
Go tell thy Lady, that hath sent me word
She will discard me, that I discard her,
And throw a scorn upon her, which I would not,
But that she does me wrong.

[Enter **EROTA**, and **ANTINOUS**.

EROTA
Do you not glory in your Conquest more,
To take some great man Prisoner, than to kill him?
And shall a Lady find less mercy from you,
That yields her self your Captive, and for her Ransome,
Will give the Jewel of her life, her heart,
Which she hath lockt from all men but thy self?
For shame (Antinous) throw this dulness off;
Art thou a man no where but in the field?

HYPARCHA

He must hear Drums, and Trumpets ere he sleeps,
And at this instant dreams he's in his Armour;
These iron-hearted Souldiers are so cold,
Till they be beaten to a Womans Arms,
And then they love 'em better than their own;
No Fort can hold them out.

ANTINOUS
What pity it is (Madam) that your self,
Who are all Excellence, should become so wretched,
To think on such a Wretch as Grief hath made me!
Seldome despairing men look up to Heaven,
Although it still speak to 'em in its Glories;
For when sad thoughts perplex the mind of man,
There is a Plummet in the heart that weighs,
And pulls us (living) to the dust we came from;
Did you but see the miseries you pursue,
(As I the happiness that I avoid
That doubles my afflictions) you would flye
Unto some Wilderness, or to your Grave,
And there find better Comforts than in me,
For Love and Cares can never dwell together.

EROTA
They should,
If thou hadst but my Love and I thy Cares.

ANTINOUS
What wild Beast in the Desart but would be
Taught by this Tongue to leave his Cruelty,
Though all the beauties of the face were vail'd!
But I am savager than any Beast,
And shall be so till Decius does arrive,
Whom with so much submission I have sent
Under my hand, that if he do not bring
His Benediction back, he must to me
Be much more cruel than I to you.

EROTA
Is't but your Fathers pardon you desire?

ANTINOUS
With his love, and then nothing next that, like yours.

[Enter **DECIUS**.

EROTA
Decius is come.

ANTINOUS
O welcome Friend; if I apprehend not
Too much of joy, there's comfort in thy looks.

EROTA
There is indeed; I prithee Decius speak it.

DECIUS
How! prithee Decius! this Woman's strangely alter'd.

ANTINOUS
Why dost not speak (good friend) and tell me how
The reverend Blessing of my life receiv'd
My humble lines; wept he for joy?

DECIUS
No, there's a Letter will inform you more;
Yet I can tell you what I think will grieve you,
The Old Man is in want and angry still,
And poverty is the Bellows to the Coal
More than distaste from you as I imagine.

ANTINOUS
What's here? how's this? It cannot be! now sure
My griefs delude my senses.

EROTA
In his looks
I read a world of Changes; Decius, mark
With what a sad amazement he surveys
The News; canst thou guess what 'tis?

DECIUS
None good, I fear.

EROTA
I fear so too; and then—

ANTINOUS
It is her hand.

EROTA
Are you not well?

ANTINOUS
Too well: if I were ought
But Rock, this Letter would conclude my miseries,

Peruse it (Lady) and resolve me then,
In what a case I stand.

DECIUS
Sir, the worst is,
Your Fathers lowness and distaste.

ANTINOUS
No, Decius,
My Sister writes Fernando has made suit
For love to her; and to express sincerely
His constant truth, hath like a noble Gentleman,
Discovered plots of treachery; contriv'd
By false Gonzalo, not intending more
The utter ruine of our house, than generally
Candies Confusion.

DECIUS
'Tis a generous part
Of young Fernando.

ANTINOUS
'Tis, and I could wish
All thrift to his affections, Decius.
You find the sum on't, Madam.

EROTA
Yes, I do.

ANTINOUS
And can you now yet think a heart opprest
With such a throng of cares, can entertain
An amorous thought? Love frees all toils but one,
Calamity and it can ill agree.

EROTA
Wil't please you speak my doom?

ANTINOUS
Alas, great Lady,
Why will you flatter thus a desperate Man
That is quite cast away? O had you not
Procur'd the Senates Warrant to enforce
My stay, I had not heard of these sad News.
What would ye have me do?

EROTA
Love me, or kill me,

One word shall sentence either; for as Truth
Is just, if you refuse me, I am resolute
Not to out-live my thraldome.

ANTINOUS
Gentle Lady.

EROTA
Say, must I live, or dye?

DECIUS
My Lord, how can you
Be so inexorable? here's Occasion
Of succouring your Father in his wants
Securely profer'd, pray Sir, entertain it.

EROTA
What is my sentence?

ANTINOUS
What you please to have it.

EROTA
As thou art gentle speak those words again.

ANTINOUS
Madam, you have prevail'd; yet give me leave
Without offence, ere I resign the interest
Your heart hath in my heart, to prove your secresie.

EROTA
Antinous, 'tis the greatest argument
Of thy affections to me.

ANTINOUS
Madam, thus then,
My Father stands for certain sums engag'd
To treacherous Gonzalo; and has morgag'd
The greatest part of his estate to him;
If you receive this Morgage, and procure
Acquittance from Gonzalo to my Father,
I am what you would have me be.

EROTA
You'll love me then?

ANTINOUS
Provided (Madam) that my Father know not

I am an Agent for him.

EROTA
If I fail
In this, I am unworthy to be lov'd.

ANTINOUS
Then (with your favour) thus I seal my truth,
To day, and Decius witness how unchangingly
I shall still love Erota.

EROTA
Thou hast quickned
A dying heart, Antinous.

DECIUS
This is well;
Much happiness to both.

[Enter **HYPARCHA**.

HYPARCHA
The Lord Gonzalo
Attends you, Madam.

EROTA
Comes as we could wish,
Withdraw Antinous, here's a Closet, where
You may partake his errand; let him enter.

[Enter **GONZALO**.

ANTINOUS
Madam you must be wary.

[Exit.

EROTA
Fear it not,
I will be ready for him; to entertain him
With smiling Welcome. Noble Sir, you take
Advantage of the time; it had been fit
Some notice of your presence might have fashion'd
A more prepared state.

GONZALO
Do you mock me, Madam?

EROTA

Trust me, you wrong your judgment, to repute
My Gratitude a fault; I have examin'd
Your portly carriage, and will now confess
It hath not slightly won me.

GONZALO

The Wind's turn'd;
I thought 'twould come to this; it pleas'd us, Madam,
At our last interview, to mention Love;
Have you consider'd on't?

EROTA

With more than common
Content: but Sir, if what you spoke you meant,
(As I have cause to doubt) then—

GONZALO

What, (sweet Lady?)

EROTA

Methinks we should lay by this form of stateliness;
Loves Courtship is familiar, and for instance,
See what a change it hath begot in me,
I could talk humbly now, as Lovers use.

GONZALO

And I, and I, we meet in one self-centre
Of blest Consent.

EROTA

I hope my weakness, Sir,
Shall not deserve neglect; but if it prove so
I am not the first Lady has been ruin'd
By being too credulous; you will smart for't one day.

GONZALO

Angel-like Lady, let me be held a Villain,
If I love not sincerely.

EROTA

Would I knew it.

GONZALO

Make proof by any fit Command.

EROTA

What, do you mean to marry me?

GONZALO
How! mean? nay more, I mean
To make you Empress of my Earthly Fortunes,
Regent of my desires, for did you covet
To be a real Queen, I could advance you.

EROTA
Now I perceive you slight me, and would make me
More simple than my Sexes frailty warrants.

GONZALO
But say your mind, and you shall be a Queen.

EROTA
On those Conditions, call me yours.

GONZALO
Enough.
But are we safe?

EROTA
Assuredly.

GONZALO
In short,
Yet, Lady, first be plain; would you not chuse
Much rather to prefer your own Sun-rising,
Than any's else though ne'r so near entituled
By Blood, or right of Birth?

EROTA
'Tis a question
Needs not a resolution.

GONZALO
Good; what if
I set the Crown of Candy on your head?

EROTA
I were a Queen indeed then.

GONZALO
Madam, know
There's but a Boy 'twixt you and it; suppose him
Transhap'd into an Angel.

EROTA

Wise Gonzalo,
I cannot but admire thee.

GONZALO
'Tis worth thinking on;
Besides, your Husband shall be Duke of Venice.

EROTA
Gonzalo, Duke of Venice?

GONZALO
You are mine you say?

EROTA
Pish: you but dally with me; and would lull me
In a rich golden dream.

GONZALO
You are too much distrustfull of my truth.

EROTA
Then you must give me leave to apprehend
The means, and manner how.

GONZALO
Why thus—

EROTA
You shall not,
We may be over-heard; Affairs and counsels
Of such high nature, are not to be trusted
Not to the Air it self, you shall in writing,
Draw out the full design; which if effected,
I am as I profess.

GONZALO
O I applaud
Your ready care, and secresie.

EROTA
Gonzalo,
There is a bar yet, 'twixt our hopes and us,
And that must be remov'd.

GONZALO
What is't?

EROTA

Old Cassilane.

GONZALO
Ha? fear not him: I build upon his ruines
Already.

EROTA
I would find a smoother course
To shift him off.

GONZALO
As how?

EROTA
We'l talk in private,
I have a ready plot.

GONZALO
I shall adore you.

[Exeunt.

[Enter **FERNANDO** and **ANNOPHEL**.

FERNANDO
Madam, although I hate unnoble practices,
And therefore have perform'd no more than what
I ought, for honours safety: yet Annophel,
Thy love hath been the spur, to urge me forward
For speedier diligence.

ANNOPHEL
Sir your own fame
And memory will best reward themselves.

FERNANDO
All gain is loss (sweet beauty) if I miss
My comforts here: The Brother and the Sister
Have double conquer'd me, but thou maist triumph.

ANNOPHEL
Good Sir, I have a Father.

FERNANDO
Yes, a brave one;
Could'st thou obscure thy beauty, yet the happiness
Of being but his Daughter, were a dower
Fit for a Prince: what say ye?

ANNOPHEL
You have deserv'd
As much as I should grant.

FERNANDO
By this fair hand
I take possession.

ANNOPHEL
What in words I dare not,
Imagine in my silence.

FERNANDO
Thou art all vertue.

[Enter **CASSILANES** and **ARCANES**.

CASSILANES
I'le tell thee how: Baldwin the Emperour,
Pretending title, more through tyranny,
Than right of conquest, or descent, usurp'd
The stile of Lord o're all the Grecian Islands,
And under colour of an amity
With Creet, prefer'd the Marquess Mountferato
To be our Governor; the Cretians vex'd
By the ambitious Turks, in hope of aid
From the Emperour, receiv'd for General,
This Mountferato; he (the wars appeased)
Plots with the state of Venice and takes money
Of them for Candy: they paid well, he steals
Away in secret; since which time, that right
The state of Venice claims o're Candy, is
By purchase, not inheritance or Conquest:
And hence grows all our quarrel.

ARCANES
So an Usurer
Or Lumbard-Jew, might with some bags of trash,
Buy half the Western world.

CASSILANES
Mony, Arcanes,
Is now a God on Earth: it cracks virginities,
And turns a Christian, Turk;
Bribes justice, cut-throats honour, does what not?

ARCANES

Not captives Candy.

CASSILANES
Nor makes thee dishonest,
Nor me a Coward—Now Sir, here is homely,
But friendly entertainment.

FERNANDO
Sir, I find it.

ARCANES
And like it, do ye not?

FERNANDO
My repair speaks for me.

CASSILANES
Fernando we are speaking off—how this?

[Enter **GONZALO** and **GASPERO** with a Casket

GONZALO
Your friend, and servant.

CASSILANES
Creditors, my Lord,
Are Masters and no Servants: as the world goes,
Debters are very slaves to those to whom
They have been beholding to; in which respect,
I should fear you Gonzalo.

GONZALO
Me, my Lord?
You owe me nothing.

CASSILANES
What, nor love, nor mony?

GONZALO
Yes, love, I hope, not mony.

CASSILANES
All this braverie
Will scarcely make that good.

GONZALO
'Tis done already:
See Sir, your Mortgage which I only took,

In case you and your son had in the wars
Miscarried: I yield it up again: 'tis yours.

CASSILANES
Are ye so conscionable?

GONZALO
'Tis your own.

CASSILANES
Pish, pish, I'le not receive what is not mine,
That were a dangerous business.

GONZALO
Sir, I am paid for't,
The summes you borrowed, are return'd; The bonds
Cancel'd, and your acquittance formerly seal'd:
Look here Sir, Gaspero is witness to it.

GASPERO
My honoured Lord, I am.

GONZALO
My Lord Fernando,
Arcanes and the rest, you all shall testifie,
That I acquit Lord Cassilane for ever,
Of any debts to me.

GASPERO
'Tis plain and ample:
Fortune will once again smile on us fairly.

CASSILANES
But hark ye, hark ye, if you be in earnest,
Whence comes this bounty? or whose is't?

GONZALO
In short,
The great Erota by this Secretary,
Return'd me my full due.

CASSILANES
Erota? why
Should she do this?

GONZALO
You must ask her the cause,
She knows it best.

CASSILANES
So ho, Arcanes, none
But women pity us? soft-hearted women?
I am become a brave fellow now, Arcanes,
Am I not?

ARCANES
Why Sir, if the gracious Princess
Have took more special notice of your services,
And means to be more thankfull than some others,
It were an injury to gratitude,
To disesteem her favours.

ANNOPHEL
Sir she ever
For your sake most respectively lov'd me.

CASSILANES
The Senate, and the body of this Kingdom
Are herein (let me speak it without arrogance)
Beholding to her: I will thank her for it;
And if she have reserv'd a means whereby
I may repay this bounty with some service,
She shall be then my Patroness: come Sirs,
We'l taste a cup of wine together now.

GONZALO
Fernando, I must speak with you in secret.

FERNANDO
You shall—Now Gaspero, all's well.

GASPERO
There's news
You must be acquainted with.
Come, there is no master-piece in Art, like Policie.

[Exeunt.

ACTUS QUINTUS

SCÆNA PRIMA

Enter **FERNANDO** and **MICHAEL**.

FERNANDO
The Senate is inform'd at full.

MICHAEL
Gonzalo
Dreams not of my arrival yet.

FERNANDO
Nor thinks
'Tis possible his plots can be discover'd:
He fats himself with hopes of Crowns, and Kingdoms,
And laughs securely, to imagine how
He means to gull all but himself: when truly,
None is so grosly gull'd as he.

MICHAEL
There was never
A more arch villain.

FERNANDO
Peace, the Senate comes.

[Enter **PORPHICIO, POSSENNE, SENATORS** and **GASPERO, ATTENDANTS.**

PORPHYCIO
How closely Treason cloaks it self in forms
Of Civil honesty!

POSSENNE
And yet how palpably
Does heaven reveal it!

FERNANDO
Gracious Lords.

GASPERO
The Embassadour,
Lord Paulo Michael, Advocate
To the great Duke of Venice.

PORPHYCIO
You are most welcome,
Your Master is a just and noble Prince.

MICHAEL
My Lords, he bad me say, that you may know
How much he scorns, and (as good Princes ought)
Defies base indirect, and godless treacheries;

To your more Sacred wisdomes he refers
The punishment due to the false Gonzalo,
Or else to send him home to Venice.

POSSENNE
Herein
The Duke is royal: Gaspero, the Prince
Of Cyprus answer'd he would come.

GASPERO
My Lords,
He will not long be absent.

[Enter **PHILANDER** and **MELITUS**.

PORPHYCIO
You Fernando,
Have made the State your debter: worthy Prince,
We shall be sutors to you for your presence,
In hearing, and determining of matters
Greatly concerning Candy.

PHILANDER
Fathers, I am
A stranger.

POSSENNE
Why, the cause, my Lord, concerns
A stranger: please you seat your self.

PHILANDER
How e're
Unfit, since you will have it so, my Lords,
You shall command me.

PORPHYCIO
You my Lord Fernando,
With the Ambassador, withdraw a while.

FERNANDO
My Lords, we shall.

[Exit.

POSSENNE
Melitus, and the Secretary,
Give notice to Gonzalo, that the Senate
Requires his presence.

[Exit **GASPERO** and **MELITUS**.

[Enter **CASSILANES** and **ARCANES**.

PHILANDER
What concerns the business?

PORPHYCIO
Thus noble Prince—

CASSILANES
Let me alone, thou troublest me,
I will be heard.

ARCANES
You know not what you do.

POSSENNE
Forbear: who's he that is so rude? what's he that dares
To interrupt our counsels?

CASSILANES
One that has guarded,
Those Purple robes from Cankers worse than Moths,
One that hath kept your fleeces on your backs,
That would have been snatch'd from you: but I see
'Tis better now to be a Dog, a Spaniel
In times of Peace, then boast the bruised scars,
Purchas'd with loss of bloud in noble wars,
My Lords, I speak to you.

PORPHYCIO
Lord Cassilane,
We know not what you mean.

CASSILANES
Yes, you are set
Upon a bench of justice; and a day
Will come (hear this, and quake ye potent great ones)
When you your selves shall stand before a judge,
Who in a pair of scales will weigh your actions,
Without abatement of one grain: as then
You would be found full weight, I charge ye fathers
Let me have justice now.

POSSENNE
Lord Cassilane,

What strange distemperature provokes distrust
Of our impartiality? be sure
We'l flatter no mans injuries.

CASSILANES
'Tis well;
You have a Law, Lords, that without remorse
Dooms such as are belepred with the curse
Of foul ingratitude unto death.

PORPHYCIO
We have.

CASSILANES
Then do me justice.

[Enter **ANTINOUS, DECIUS, EROTA, HYPARCHA.**

DECIUS
Mad-man, whither run'st thou?

ANTINOUS
Peace Decius, I am deaf.

HYPARCHA
Will you forget
Your greatness, and your modesty?

EROTA HYPARCHA
leave, I will not hear.

ANTINOUS
Lady; great, gentle, Lady.

EROTA
Prethee young man forbear to interrupt me,
Triumph not in thy fortunes; I will speak.

POSSENNE
More uproars yet! who are they that disturb us?

CASSILANES
The viper's come; his fears have drawn him hither,
And now, my Lords, be Chronicled for ever,
And give me justice against this vile Monster,
This bastard of my bloud.

EROTA

'Tis justice, Fathers,
I sue for too: and though I might command it,
(If you remember Lords, whose child I was)
Yet I will humbly beg it; this old wretch
Has forfeited his life to me.

CASSILANES
Tricks, tricks;
Complots, devices, 'twixt these pair of young-ones,
To blunt the edge of your well temper'd Swords,
Wherewith you strike offenders, Lords, but I
Am not a baby to be fear'd with bug-bears,
'Tis justice I require.

EROTA
And I.

ANTINOUS
You speak too tenderly; and too much like yourself
To mean a cruelty; which would make monstrous
Your Sex: yet for the loves sake, which you once
Pleas'd to pretend, give my griev'd Father leave
To urge his own revenge; you have no cause
For yours: keep peace about ye.

CASSILANES
Will you hear me?

PHILANDER
Here's some strange novelty.

POSSENNE
Sure we are mock'd,
Speak one at once: say wherein hath your Son
Transgress'd the Law?

CASSILANES
O the gross mists of dulness!
Are you this Kingdomes Oracles, yet can be
So ignorant? first hear, and then consider.
That I begot him, gave him birth and life,
And education, were, I must confess,
But duties of a Father: I did more;
I taught him how to manage Arms, to dare
An Enemy; to court both death and dangers;
Yet these were but additions to compleat
A well accomplish'd Souldier: I did more yet.
I made him chief Commander in the field

Next to my self, and gave him the full prospeft
Of honour, and preferment; train'd him up
In all perfections of a Martiallist:
But he unmindful of his gratitude,
You know with what contempt of my deserts,
First kick'd against mine honour, scorned all
My services; then got the palm of glory
Unto himself: yet not content with this,
He (lastly) hath conspir'd my death, and sought
Means to engage me to this Lady's debt,
Whose bounty all my whole estate could never
Give satisfaction to: now honoured Fathers,
For this cause only, if your Law be law,
And you the Ministers of justice; then
Think of this strange ingratitude in him.

PHILANDER
Can this be so Antinous?

ANTINOUS
'Tis all true,
Nor hath my much wrong'd father limn'd my faults
In colours half so black, as in themselves,
My guilt hath dy'd them: were there mercy left,
Yet mine own shame would be my Executioner:
Lords, I am guilty.

EROTA
Thou beliest, Antinous,
Thine innocence: alas, my Lords, he's desperate,
And talks he knows not what: you must not credit
His lunacy; I can my self disprove
This accusation: Cassilane, be yet
More mercifull; I beg it.

CASSILANES
Time, not fate,
The world, or what is in it, shall not alter
My resolution: he shall dye.

EROTA
The Senats
Prayers, or weeping Lovers, shall not alter
My resolution: thou shalt dye.

ANTINOUS
Why Madam,
Are ye all Marble?

POSSENNE
Leave your shifts Antinous,
What plead you to your Fathers accusation?

ANTINOUS
Most fully guilty.

POSSENNE
You have doom'd your self,
We cannot quit you now.

CASSILANES
A burthen'd conscience
Will never need a hang-man: hadst thou dar'd
To have deni'd it, then this Sword of mine
Should on thy head have prov'd thy tongue a lyar.

EROTA
Thy sword? wretched old man, thou hast liv'd too long
To carry peace or comfort to thy grave;
Thou art a man condemn'd: my Lords, this tyrant
Had perish'd but for me, I still suppli'd
His miserable wants; I sent his Daughter
Mony to buy him food; the bread he eat,
Was from my purse: when he (vain-gloriously)
To dive into the peoples hearts, had pawn'd
His birth-right, I redeem'd it, sent it to him,
And for requitall, only made my suite,
That he would please to new receive his son
Into his favour, for whose love I told him
I had been still so friendly: but then he
As void of gratitude, as all good nature,
Distrafted like a mad man, poasted hither
To pull this vengeance on himself, and us;
For why, my Lords, since by the Law, all means
Is blotted out of your commission,
As this hard hearted Father hath accus'd
Noble Antinous, his unblemished Son,
So I accuse this Father, and crave judgement.

CASSILANES
All this is but deceit, meer trifles forg'd
By combination to defeat the process
Of Justice, I will have Antinous life.

ARCANES
Sir, what do ye mean?

EROTA

I will have Cassilane's.

ANTINOUS

Cunning and cruel Lady, runs the stream
Of your affections this way? have you not
Conquest enough by treading on my grave?
Unless you send me thither in a shrowd
Steept in my fathers bloud? as you are woman,
As the protests of love you vow'd were honest;
Be gentler to my Father.

EROTA

Cassilane,
Thou hast a heart of flint: let my intreaties,
My tears, the Sacrifice of griefs unfeigned,
Melt it: yet be a Father to thy son,
Unmask thy long besotted judgement, see
A low obedience kneeling at the feet
Of nature, I beseech you.

CASSILANES

Pish, you cozen
Your hopes: your plots are idle: I am resolute.

EROTA

Antinous, urge no further.

ANTINOUS

Hence thou Sorcery
Of a beguiling softness, I will stand,
Like the earths center, unmov'd; Lords your breath
Must finish these divisions: I confess
Civility doth teach I should not speak
Against a Lady of her birth, so high
As great Erota, but her injuries
And thankless wrongs to me, urge me to cry
Aloud for justice, Fathers.

DECIUS

Whither run you?

ANTINOUS

For (honoured fathers) that you all may know
That I alone am not unmatchable
In crimes of this condition, lest perhaps
You might conceive, as yet the case appears,

That this foul stain, and guilt runs in a bloud;
Before this presence, I accuse this Lady
Of as much vile ingratitude to me.

CASSILANES
Impudent Traitor!

PHILANDER
Her? O spare Antinous;
The world reputes thee valiant, do not soyle
All thy past nobleness with such a cowardize.
As murthering innocent Ladies will stamp on thee.

ANTINOUS
Brave Prince, with what unwillingness I force
Her follies, and in those her sin, be witness,
All these about me: she is bloudy minded,
And turns the justice of the Law to rigor:
It is her cruelites, not I accuse her:
Shall I have Audience?

EROTA
Let him speak my Lords.

DECIUS
Your memory will rot.

ANTINOUS
Cast all your eyes
On this, what shall I call her? truthless woman,
When often in my discontents, the sway
Of her unruly bloud, her untam'd passion,
(Or name it as you list) had hour by hour
Solicited my love, she vow'd at last
She could not, would not live unless I granted
What she long sued for: I in tender pity,
To save a Lady of her birth from ruine,
Gave her her life, and promis'd to be hers:
Nor urg'd I ought from her, but secresie,
And then enjoyn'd her to supply such wants
As I perceiv'd my Fathers late engagements
Had made him subject to; what shall I heap up
Long repetitions? she to quit my pity,
Not only hath discover'd to my Father
What she had promis'd to conceal, but also
Hath drawn my life into this fatal forfeit;
For which since I must dye, I crave a like
Equality of justice against her;

Not that I covet bloud, but that she may not
Practise this art of falsehood on some other,
Perhaps more worthy of her love hereafter.

PORPHYCIO
If this be true—

EROTA
My Lords, be as the Law is,
Indifferent, upright, I do plead guilty:
Now Sir, what glory have you got by this?
'Las man, I meant not to outlive thy doom,
Shall we be friends in death?

CASSILANES
Hear me, the villain
Scandals her, honour'd Lords.

EROTA
Leave off to doat,
And dye a wise man.

ANTINOUS
I am over-reach'd,
And master'd in my own resolution.

PHILANDER
Will ye be wilfull Madam? here's the curse
Of loves disdain.

CASSILANES
Why sit you like dumb Statues?
Demur no longer.

POSSENNE
Cassilane, Erota,
Antinous, death ye ask; and 'tis your dooms,
You in your follies liv'd, dye in your follies.

CASSILANES
I am reveng'd, and thank you for it.

EROTA
Yes, and I: Antinous hath been gracious.

ANTINOUS
Sir, may I presume to crave a blessing from you
Before we part?

CASSILANES
Yes, such a one as Parents
Bestow on cursed sons, now now, I laugh
To see how those poor younglings are both cheated
Of life and comfort: look ye, look ye, Lords,
I go but some ten minutes (more or less)
Before my time, but they have finely cozen'd
Themselves of many, many hopefull years
Amidst their prime of youth and glory; now

[Enter **ANNOPHEL**.

My vengeance is made full. Welcom my joy,
Thou com'st to take a seasonable blessing
From thy half buried Fathers hand; I am dead
Already girle, and so is she and he,
We all are worms-meat now.

ANNOPHEL
I have heard all;
Nor shall you dye alone: Lords on my knees
I beg for justice too.

PORPHYCIO
'Gainst whom, for what?

ANNOPHEL
First let me be resolv'd; does the Law favour
None, be they ne're so mighty?

PORPHYCIO
Not the greatest.

ANNOPHEL
Then justly I accuse of foul ingratitude
My Lords, you of the Senate all, not one
Excepted.

POSSENNE PORPHYCIO
Us?

PHILANDER
Annophel—

ANNOPHEL
You are the Authors
Of this unthrifty bloud-shed; when your enemies

Came marching to your gates, your children suck'd not
Safe at their Mothers breasts, your very Cloysters
Were not secure, your starting-holes of refuge
Not free from danger, nor your lives your own:
In this most desperate Ecstasie, my Father,
This aged man, not only undertook
To guard your lives, but did so; and beat off
The daring foe; for you he pawn'd his lands,
To pay your Souldiers, who without their pay
Refus'd to strike a blow: but, Lords, when peace
Was purchas'd for you, and victorie brought home,
Where was your gratitude, who in your Coffers
Hoarded the rustic treasure which was due
To my unminded Father? he was glad
To live retir'd in want, in penurie,
Whilst you made feasts of surfeit, and forgot
Your debts to him: The sum of all is this,
You have been unthankfull to him; and I crave
The rigor of the Law against you all.

CASSILANES
My Royal spirited daughter!

EROTA
Annophel
Thou art a worthy wench; let me embrace thee.

ANNOPHEL
Lords, why do ye keep your seats? they are no places
For such as are offenders.

POSSENNE
Though our ignorance
Of Cassilanes engagements might asswage
Severity of justice, yet to shew
How no excuse should smooth a breach of Law,
I yield me to the trial of it.

PORPHYCIO
So must I:
Great Prince of Cyprus, you are left
The only Moderator in this difference;
And as you are a Prince be a Protector
To wofull Candy.

PHILANDER
What a Scene of miserie
Hath thine obdurate frowardness (old man)

Drawn on thy Countries bosom? and for that
Thy proud ambition could not mount so high
As to be stil'd thy Countries only Patron,
Thy malice hath descended to the depth
Of Hell, to be renowned in the Title
Of the destroyer? dost thou yet perceive
What curses all posterity will brand
Thy grave with? that at once hast rob'd this Kingdom
Of honour and of safety.

EROTA
Children yet unborn
Will stop their ears when thou art nam'd.

ARCANES
The world will be too little to contain
The memorie of this detested deed;
The Furies will abhorr it.

DECIUS
What the sword
Could not enforce, your peevish thirst of honour
(A brave, cold, weak, imaginarie fame)
Hath brought on Candy: Candy groans, not these
That are to die.

PHILANDER
'Tis happiness enough
For them, that they shall not survive to see
The wounds wherewith thou stab'st the land that gave
Thee life and name.

DECIUS
'Tis Candy's wrack shall feel—

CASSILANES
The mischief of your folly.

PORPHYCIO & **POSSENNE**
Annophel—

ANNOPHEL
I will not be entreated.

CASSILANES
Prethee Annophel.

ANNOPHEL

Why would ye urge me to a mercy which
You in your self allow not?

CASSILANES
'Tis the Law,
That if the party who complains, remit
The offender, he is freed: is't not so Lords?

PORPHYCIO POSSENNE
'Tis so.

CASSILANES
Antinous, By my shame observe
What a close witch-craft popular applause is:
I am awak'd, and with clear eyes behold
The Lethargie wherein my reason long
Hath been be-charm'd: live, live, my matchless son,
Blest in thy Fathers blessing; much more blest
In thine own vertues: let me dew thy cheeks
With my unmanly tears: Rise, I forgive thee:
And good Antinous, if I shall be thy Father
Forgive me: I can speak no more.

ANTINOUS
Dear Sir,
You new beget me now—Madam your pardon,
I heartily remit you.

EROTA
I as freely
Discharge thee Cassilane.

ANNOPHEL
My gracious Lords,
Repute me not a blemish to my Sex,
In that I strove to cure a desperate evil
With a more violent remedy: your lives,
Your honours are your own.

PHILANDER
Then with consent
Be reconcil'd on all sides: Please you Fathers
To take your places.

POSSENNE
Let us again ascend,
With joy and thankfulness to Heaven: and now
To other business Lords.

[Enter **GASPERO**, and **MELITUS**, with **GONZALO**.

MELITUS
Two hours and more Sir,
The Senate hath been set.

GONZALO
And I not know it?
Who sits with them?

MELITUS
My Lord, the Prince of Cyprus.

GONZALO
Gaspero,
Why how comes that to pass?

GASPERO
Some weighty cause
I warrant you.

GONZALO
Now Lords the business? ha?
Who's here, Erota?

PORPHYCIO
Secretarie do your charge
Upon that Traitor.

GONZALO
Traitor?

GASPERO
Yes, Gonzalo, Traitor,
Of treason to the peace and state of Candy,
I do arrest thee.

GONZALO
Me? thou Dog?

[Enter **FERNANDO** and **MICHAEL**.

MICHAEL
With Licence
From this grave Senate, I arrest thee likewise
Of treason to the State of Venice.

GONZALO
Ha?
Is Michael here? nay then I see
I am undone.

EROTA
I shall not be your Queen,
Your Dutchess, or your Empress.

GONZALO
Dull, dull brain.
O I am fool'd!

GASPERO
Look Sir, do you know this hand?

MICHAEL
Do you know this Seal? First, Lords, he writes to Venice,
To make a perfect league, during which time
He would in private keep some Troops in pay,
Bribe all the Centinels throughout this Kingdom,
Corrupt the Captains; at a Banquet poyson
The Prince, and greatest Peers, and in conclusion
Yield Candy slave to Venice.

GASPERO
Next, he contracted
With the Illustrious Princess, the Lady Erota,
In hope of marriage with her, to deliver
All the Venetian gallantry, and strength,
Upon their first arrival, to the mercy
Of her and Candy.

EROTA
This is true, Gonzalo.

GONZALO
Let it be true: what then?

POSSENNE
My Lord Ambassadour,
What's your demand?

MICHAEL
As likes the State of Candy,
Either to sentence him as he deserves
Here, or to send him like a slave to Venice.

PORPHYCIO
We shall advise upon it.

GONZALO
O the Devils,
That had not thrust this trick into my pate—
A Politician fool? destruction plague
Candy and Venice both.

POSSENNE PORPHYCIO
Away with him.

MELITUS
Come Sir, I'le see you safe.

[Exeunt **GONZALO, MELITUS**.

EROTA
Lords, e're you part
Be witness to another change of wonder;
Antinous, now be bold, before this presence,
Freely to speak, whether or no I us'd
The humblest means affection could contrive,
To gain thy love.

ANTINOUS
Madam, I must confess it,
And ever am your servant.

EROTA
Yes Antinous,
My servant, for my Lord thou shalt be never:
I here disclaim the interest thou hadst once
In my too passionate thoughts. Most noble Prince,
If yet a relique of thy wonted flames
Live warm within thy bosom, then I blush not
To offer up the assurance of my faith,
To thee that hast deserv'd it best.

PHILANDER
O Madam,
You play with my calamity.

EROTA
Let heaven
Record my truth for ever.

PHILANDER

With more joy
Than I have words to utter, I accept it.
I also pawn you mine.

EROTA
The man that in requital
Of noble and un-sought affection
Grows cruel, never lov'd, nor did Antinous.
Yet herein (Prince) ye are beholding to him;
For his neglect of me humbled a pride,
Which to a vertuous wife had been a Monster.

PHILANDER
For which I'le rank him my deserving friend.

ANTINOUS
Much comfort dwell with you, as I could wish
To him I honour most.

CASSILANES
O my Antinous,
My own, my own good son.

FERNANDO
One suit I have to make.

PHILANDER
To whom Fernando?

FERNANDO
Lord Cassilane to you.

CASSILANES
To me?

FERNANDO
This Lady
Hath promised to be mine.

ANNOPHEL
Your blessing Sir;
Brother your love.

ANTINOUS
You cannot Sir bestow her
On a more noble Gentleman.

CASSILANES

Saist thou so?
Antinous I confirm it. Here Fernando,
Live both as one; she is thine.

ANTINOUS
And herein Sister,
I honour you for your wise setled love.
This is a day of Triumph, all Contentions
Are happily accorded: Candy's peace
Secur'd, and Venice vow'd a worthy friend.

[Exeunt.

JOHN FORD – A SHORT BIOGRAPHY

John Ford was born in 1586 in Ilsington, in Devon, the second son of Thomas Ford of Bagtor in the parish of Ilsington and his wife Elizabeth Popham (d.1629) of the Popham family of Huntworth in Somerset. (Her monument can still be found in Ilsington Church).

Thomas Ford's grandfather was also named John Ford (d.1538) of Ashburton himself the son and heir of William Ford of Chagford, who had previously purchased the estate of Bagtor in the parish of Ilsington, which his male heirs successively made their seat.

The Elizabethan mansion of the Fords still survives today at Bagtor as the service wing of a later house appended in about 1700.

John Ford is listed as being baptized on April 17th, 1586.

Details of his life are scare and some have a variance of truth about them. We have attempted to give the most plausible view of his life.

It was thought that Ford left home to study in London but a sixteen-year-old John Ford of Devon was admitted to Exeter College in Oxford on 26 March 1601, but Ford could only have been fifteen at this time and, whatever the truth, endured only a short university life.

By 1602 Ford, had by most accounts, been admitted to Middle Temple in London, a prestigious law school but also a centre for literary and dramatic pursuits. Intriguingly whether he actually studied Law is unknown. A common arrangement at the time was to attend as a 'gentleman boarder'.

In 1606 Ford was expelled due to his financial problems. He then wrote and had published two poems Fame's Memorial and Honour Triumphant.

Both works seem to have been written in the hopes of gaining a patron. Fame's Memorial is a long elegy, composed of 1169 lines, on the recently deceased Charles Blount, 1st Earl of Devonshire. Honour Triumphant is a prose pamphlet, a verbal fantasia written in connection with the jousts planned for the summer 1606 visit of King Christian IV of Denmark.

Whether either of these brought any financial remuneration to Ford is unknown; yet by June 1608 he had acquired sufficient funds to be readmitted to the Middle Temple where he would remain until 1617, and possibly later.

During this second period at Middle Temple Ford continued to generate non-dramatic works. In 1613 the long religious poem, Christ's Bloody Sweat, (1613), was followed by two more prose pieces which were published as essays; The Golden Mean, in that same year of 1613 and A Line of Life, several years later in 1620.

By this time he had left Middle Temple and was to actively begin writing for the Theatre.

His initial forays into playwriting began with other more senior and well-known collaborators such as Thomas Dekker, John Webster, and William Rowley. It is difficult to distinguish the share of the writing amongst them but certainly his themes, style, rhythm and language are at least an influence and undoubtedly grew with each production.

From about 1627 to 1638 Ford wrote plays by himself, mostly for private theatres, but the sequence of his eight surviving plays cannot be absolutely determined, and only two of them can be dated with certainty.

The first play, written wholly by Ford, and as importantly still in existence (much of his canon unfortunately has been lost and is, in its own way, a tragedy to the culture of these shores) is The Lover's Melancholy (1629).

However it is his most famous work 'Tis Pity She's a Whore, printed in 1633, where in the Prologue, Ford declares the play as "the first fruits of his leisure." Whether success dictated that statement or not it became his most well regarded, admired and most popular work.

1633 appears to have been a very important year for Ford. Two other of his plays were also printed - The Broken Heart and Love's Sacrifice.

Ford's outstanding reputation, is set mainly with his first four plays in which he was the sole author. Of these, 'Tis Pity She's a Whore is the most powerful. The narrative tells of, for the time, shocking tale of the incestuous love of Giovanni and his sister Annabella. When she is found to be pregnant, she agrees to marry her suitor Soranzo. The lovers' secret is finally discovered, but Soranzo's plan for revenge is outpaced by Giovanni's murder of Annabella and then Soranzo, at the hands of whose hired killers Giovanni himself finally dies.

Whilst Ford is clearly sympathetic to his protagonists he is in no way arguing any case for the brother and sister's unnatural union, but explores their isolation. Because of this unlawful relationship, their consciousness of their sin, and their sensual and at times even arrogant acceptance of it become a compelling part of the work.

With The Broken Heart Ford's virtuous heroine is involved in the timeless tale of having to choose between her true love and an unhappy forced marriage, again with tragic consequences for all concerned.

In his historical play The Chronicle History of Perkin Warbeck from 1634, the central theme is of a deluded impostor of that same name who claims to be the Duke of York.

The Lover's Melancholy is the best of Ford's other plays, all of which are tragicomedies.

Ford's austerely powerful themes are set off by subplots with minor characters and perhaps not the greatest of comedy, but together they outline him as the most important tragedian of the reign of King Charles I (1625–49).

His work is further distinguished by the highly wrought power of his blank verse and by characters, who are all frustrated and whose desires and efforts are stymied and, more often than not, are shut out by the dictates of circumstance.

In 1638 The Fancies Chaste and Noble was published and in the following year so was his final play, The Lady's Trial.

There is some evidence that Ford had married, the union producing several children. But there is nothing written after 1639 which is the year he is presumed to have died at his paternal home, the manor-house at Ilsington.

He I revered today as a major playwright of the reign of Caroline era. His plays deal with conflicts between individual passion and conscience and the laws and morals of society at large, much of which is understood and still relevant to audiences today.

As mentioned before little is known of his personal life but his legacy with the works that have survived detail an immense contribution to the literary life of England. Certainly he was the most important playwright of his generation and has left a standard that few have and few others will achieve.

JOHN FORD – A CONCISE BIBLIOGRAPHY

Plays
The Witch of Edmonton (1621; printed 1658), with Thomas Dekker and William Rowley
The Sun's Darling (licensed 3 March 1624; revised 1638–39; printed 1656), with Thomas Dekker
The Lover's Melancholy (licensed 24 November 1628; printed 1629)
The Broken Heart (ca. 1625–33; printed 1633)
Love's Sacrifice (1632; printed 1633)
'Tis Pity She's a Whore (1629–33; printed 1633)
The Chronicle History of Perkin Warbeck (ca. 1629–34; printed 1634), with Thomas Dekker
The Fancies Chaste and Noble (1635-6; printed 1638)
The Lady's Trial (licensed 3 May 1638; printed 1639)
The Laws of Candy (Printed 1647 and attributed then to John Fletcher)

It seems highly probably that Ford wrote the following:-

The Queen (ca. 1621–33; printed 1653)

The Spanish Gypsy (licensed 9 July 1623; printed 1653) attributed to Thomas Middleton & William Rowley.

Several others are lost and cannot be dated but include:-

The Royal Combat
Beauty in a Trance
The London Merchant, with Thomas Dekker
The Bristol Merchant, with Thomas Dekker
The Fairy Knight, with Thomas Dekker
Keep the Widow Waking, with William Rowley and John Webster.

And there are possible or questionable attributions:

The Welsh Ambassador by Thomas Dekker likewise may contain Ford's work
The Fair Maid of the Inn, by Thomas Dekker, in part at least, contains some work by Ford.

There may possibly be parts of his work in other plays by Francis Beaumont and John Fletcher.

In 1940, critic Alfred Harbage argued that Sir Robert Howard's play The Great Favourite, or The Duke of Lerma is an adaptation of a lost play by Ford. Harbage noted that many previous critics had judged the play suspiciously good, too good for Howard; and Harbage pointed to a range of resemblances between the play and Ford's work.

Ford was also a noted poet though few works remain

Poems & Essays
Fame's Memorial (1606)
Honour Triumphant (1606)
Christ's Bloody Sweat (1613)
The Golden Mean (1613)
A Line of Life (1620)

PHILIP MASSINGER – A SHORT BIOGRAPHY

This biography was initially written in 1830

Very few materials exist for a life of Massinger beyond the entries of the Parish Register or the College Books, and a few slender intimations scattered here and there in the dedications to his plays. From these scanty sources the following brief memoir is derived.

Our author was born at Salisbury in the year 1584: he was the son of Arthur Massinger, a gentleman in the service of Henry, the second Earl of Pembroke. We must not suppose, from his being thus attached to the family of a nobleman, that the father of our poet was a person of inferior birth and station. In those days the word servant carried with it no sense of degradation. The great lords and officers of the court numbered inferior nobles among their followers. We read, in Cavendish's Life of Wolsey, that "my

Lord Percy, the son and heir of the Earl of Northumberland, attended upon and was servitor to the lord-cardinal:" and from the situation which Arthur Massinger held in the household of so high and influential a person as the Earl of Pembroke, we might be justly led to argue rather favourably than unfavourably of his family and his connexions. "There were," says Mr. Gifford, "many considerations which united to render this state of dependance respectable and even honourable. The secretaries, clerks, and assistants, of various departments, were not then, as now, nominated by the government, but left to the choice of the person who held the employment; and as no particular dwelling was officially set apart for their residence, they were entertained in the house of their principal. That communication, too, between noblemen of power and trust, both of a public and private nature, which is now committed to the post, was in those days managed by confidential servants, who were despatched from one to the other, and even to the sovereign;" and, indeed, the father of our poet himself was, we know, in one instance thus employed as the bearer of communications from his patron to Elizabeth. We read in The Sidney Letters, "Mr. Massinger is newly come up from the Earl of Pembroke with letters to the queen for his lordship's leave to be away this St. George's Day." This was an errand which would not have been intrusted to the execution of any inconsiderable person: unimportant as the occasion may appear to us, it would not have been regarded in that light by Elizabeth; for no monarch ever exacted from the nobility, and particularly from her officers of state, a more rigid and scrupulous compliance with stated order than this princess.

With regard to the early youth of Massinger, we possess no information whatever. Mr. Gifford supposes that it might have been passed at Wilton, a seat belonging to the Earl of Pembroke, in the neighbourhood of Salisbury; but this mode of disposing of his early years rests on a very improbable conjecture. It may occasionally have happened that the child of a favourite dependant was admitted as the companion of the younger branches of the patron's family, and allowed to receive his education among them; but this was certainly not an ordinary case; and, like Cavendish, a large majority of the great man's servants and dependants "left wife and children, home and family, rest and quietness, only to serve him."—Massinger was most likely educated at the grammar-school of Salisbury, where many distinguished characters have received the rudiments of their education, among whom the elegant and accomplished Addison is to be numbered. But wherever the first years of our poet's life may have been spent, and whatever may have been the nature of his education, we know that at the age of eighteen (May 14, 1602) he was entered at the university of Oxford, and became a commoner of St. Alban's Hall.

Massinger resided at Oxford about four years, and then abruptly left it, without taking any degree. The cause of this sudden departure is ascribed by Mr. Gifford to the death of his father, from whom his supplies were derived: but Davies relates a very different story, and asserts that the Earl of Pembroke, who had sent him to the university and maintained him there, withdrew the necessary allowance in consequence of his having misapplied the time demanded for severer studies, in the pursuit of a more attractive but less profitable description of literature. Each opinion is equally ungrounded on the basis of any substantial evidence, and rests almost entirely on the imagination of the biographer: what slight authority there is favours the latter supposition, which, perhaps, on the whole, is most consistent with the known circumstances of the case. Anthony Wood, who was born, lived, and died at Oxford; who spent his time in collecting and recording the gossip which circulated in the university respecting the characters and conduct of its more distinguished sons; and whose evidence, however indifferent it may be, is the best that can be obtained upon the subject, confirms the representation of Davies:—"Massinger," says Wood, "gave his mind more to poetry and romance, for about four years or more, than to logic and philosophy, which he ought to have done, as he was patronised to that end." This passage corroborates the account of Davies so far as to intimate that patronage was afforded to our author, and that cause of dissatisfaction was given to the patron; but it goes no farther: it does not even state to whom the poet was indebted for assistance, nor that the misapplication of his academic hours was at all resented by the friend from whom the assistance was received: but still Wood is very probably correct in his information that other than his paternal funds were depended upon for maintaining Massinger at the university; and if such was the case, there can be no question from whose hands they must have proceeded; while the simple fact of his having been totally neglected, from the time of his father's death, by the whole of the Pembroke family, till after the demise of the earl, carries with it a strong suspicion that some offence was committed on the side of the poet, and tenaciously remembered on the side of the peer. Henry, the second Earl of Pembroke, died (1601) the year before Massinger was admitted at Oxford; and William, the third earl, to whom the father of Massinger continued attached during life, is universally and justly considered one of the brightest ornaments of the courts of Elizabeth and James. He was a man of generous and liberal disposition; the distinguished patron of arts and learning; and a lover of poetry, which he himself cultivated with some degree of success. It is not probable—it is impossible—that such a man should have allowed the highly talented son of an old and faithful servant of his family to be checked in his course of study, and abandoned to maintain, through the early years of life, a single-handed contest with adversity, for the want of that pecuniary aid which he could have yielded and never missed, unless some strong and decided cause of displeasure had existed. Had Massinger been merely forced to leave the university, as Mr. Gifford supposes, because the funds necessary to maintain him there had failed with the life of his father, we impute an act of illiberality to the Earl of Pembroke which is inconsistent with the whole tenor of his life and character. From whatever source the expenses of our author's education were originally defrayed, their suddenly ceasing argues in favour of the account intimated by Wood and detailed by Davies. If his father had, during his life, supported him at the university, there must have been some reason for the earl's not continuing that support when the father of Massinger was no more; and perhaps the most honourable supposition for both parties is that which represents the earl as offended by the bent of our author's studies and pursuits. By adopting this view of the case we are saved from the painful necessity of either assuming, on the one hand, that a nobleman distinguished among the most amiable characters of his age allowed a highly gifted and meritorious young man, a natural dependant of his house, to languish in the want of that countenance and protection on which he had an hereditary claim; or, on the other hand, that Massinger had incurred the displeasure of his natural and hereditary patron by the commission of some more crying offence.

Every, even the slightest, surmise of Mr. Gifford is deserving attention and respect; but I cannot admit the supposition by which he would account for the alienation that subsisted between the Earl of Pembroke and our author. That distinguished critic has inferred, from the religious sentiments contained in The Virgin Martyr, that Massinger was a Roman catholic, and for that cause neglected by the protector of his father. But if the intimations scattered through this play and others should be received as sufficient evidence of the faith of Massinger, we must, on similar evidence—the intimations contained in Measure for Measure, for instance—conclude that the religion of Shakspeare was the same; and then we are cast back upon our old difficulty, and have to explain why William Earl of Pembroke, a celebrated patron of literary men, and of dramatists in particular, scorned to yield his notice to the catholic Massinger, while (to use the expression of Heminge and Condell) he "prosequuted" the catholic Shakspeare and "his works with so much favour?" There are many reasons for believing Shakspeare to have been a member of the church of Rome; and the patronage afforded him by the Earl of Pembroke proves, that that nobleman extended his liberality to men of genius without any regard to distinctions of faith; but, on the other hand, we have no just grounds for assuming that Massinger really did hold the same opinions. The only evidence we have upon this point, that afforded by the general tone of his writings, is of a most vague and superficial description. What, in fact, can be inferred from it? We may from such a source derive very satisfactory information respecting the sentiments which would be favourably received by the audience, but very little respecting those of the author. The truth is, that though the national religion was reformed in its liturgy and articles, the feelings, prejudices, and superstitions of the people were still almost entirely catholic; and Massinger, like any other dramatic author, writing for the amusement of the people, necessarily addressed them in a language they would understand, and with sentiments that accorded with their own. Besides, as a poet, he would never carry his theological distinctions to his literary labours: Voltaire himself is catholic in his tragedies; and Massinger naturally adopted the creed which was most suitable to the purposes of poetry, and afforded the most picturesque ceremonies and romantic situations. I feel inclined, therefore, to dismiss entirely the theory suggested by Mr. Gifford, for these two reasons; first, supposing our author to have been a catholic, we have no reason for condemning the Earl of Pembroke as a bigot and a persecutor, who would close his eyes to the merits of so great an author, because his faith did not tally with his own; and, secondly, we have no sufficient grounds for supposing him to have been a catholic at all. But with regard to all such visionary conjectures, thinking is literally a waste of thought.

Whatever may have been the nature of Massinger's studies at Oxford, it is quite certain, from the general character of his works, that his time could not have been wasted there; and his literary acquirements, at the period of his leaving the university, appear to have been multifarious and extensive. He was about two-and-twenty (1606) when he arrived in London, where, as he more than once observes, he was driven by his necessities, and somewhat inclined, perhaps, by the peculiar bent of his talents, to dedicate himself to the service of the stage.

The theatre, when Massinger first took up his abode in the metropolis, must have presented attractions of all others the most calculated to excite the interest, and inspire the imagination, of a young man of sensibility, taste, and education like our poet. No art ever attained a more rapid maturity than the dramatic art in England. The people had, indeed, been long accustomed to a species of exhibition, called MIRACLES or MYSTERIES, founded on sacred subjects, and performed by the ministers of religion themselves, on the holy festivals, in or near the churches, and designed to instruct the ignorant in the leading facts of sacred history. From the occasional introduction of allegorical characters, such as Faith, Death, Hope, or Sin, into these religious dramas, representations of another kind, called MORALITIES, had by degrees arisen, of which the plots were more artificial, regular, and connected, and which were entirely formed of such personifications: but the first rough draught of a regular tragedy and comedy— Lord Sackville's Gorboduc, and Still's Gammer Gurton's Needle—were not produced till within the latter half of the sixteenth century, and little more than twenty years before the stage acquired its highest splendour in the productions of Shakspeare.

About the end of the sixteenth century, the attention of the public began to be more generally directed to the drama; and it throve most admirably beneath the cheering beams of popular favour. The theatrical performances which in the early part of Elizabeth's reign had been exhibited on temporary stages, erected in such halls or apartments as the actors could procure, or, more generally, in the yards of the larger inns, while the spectators surveyed them from the surrounding windows and galleries, began to find more convenient and permanent habitations. About the year 1569, a regular playhouse, under the appropriate name of The Theatre, was erected. It is supposed to have stood somewhere in Blackfriars; and, three years after the commencement of this establishment, the queen, yielding to her own inclination for such amusements, and disregarding the remonstrances of the Puritans, granted licence and authority to the servants of the Earl of Leicester ("for the recreation of her loving subjects, as for her own solace and pleasure when she should think good to see them") to exercise their occupation throughout the whole realm of England. From this time the number of theatres increased with the increasing demands of the people. Various noblemen had their respective companies of performers, who were associated as their servants, and acted under their protection; and when Massinger left Oxford, and commenced dramatic author, there were no less than seven principal theatres open in the metropolis.

With respect to the interior arrangements, there were very few points of difference between our modern theatres and those of the days of Massinger. The prices of admission, indeed, were considerably cheaper: to the boxes the entrance was a shilling; to the pit and galleries only sixpence. Sixpence also was the price paid for stools upon the stage; and these seats, as we learn from Decker's Gull's Hornbook, were particularly affected by the wits and critics of the time. The conduct of the audience was less restrained by the sense of public decorum, and smoking tobacco, playing at cards, eating and drinking, were generally prevalent among them. The hours of performance were also earlier: the play commencing at one o'clock. During the representation a flag was unfurled at the top of the theatre; and the stage, according to the universal practice of the age, was strewn with rushes; but, in all other respects, the theatres of Elizabeth and James's days seem to have borne a perfect resemblance to our own. They had their pit, where the inferior class of spectators, the groundlings, vented their clamorous censure or approbation; they had their boxes—rooms as they were called—to which the right of exclusive admission was engaged by the night, for the more affluent portion of the audience; and there were again the galleries, or scaffoldings above the boxes, for those who were content to purchase less commodious situations at a cheaper rate. On the stage, in the same manner, the appointments appear to have been nearly of the same description as at present. The curtain divided the audience from the actors, which, at the third sounding, not indeed of the bell, but of the trumpet, was drawn for the commencement of the performance. Malone, in his account of the ancient theatre, supposes that there were no moveable scenes; that a permanent elevation of about nine feet was raised at the back of the stage, from which, in many of the old plays, part of the dialogue was spoken; and that there was a private box on each side this platform. Such an arrangement would have destroyed all theatrical illusion; and it seems extraordinary that any spectators should desire to fix themselves in a station where they could have seen nothing but the backs and trains of the performers; but, as Malone himself acknowledges the spot to have been inconvenient, and that "it is not very easy to ascertain the precise situation where these boxes really were", it may very reasonably be presumed, that they were not placed in the position that the historian of the English stage has supposed. As to the permanent floor, or upper stage, of which he speaks, he may or may not be correct in his statement. All that his quotations upon the subject really establish is, that in the old, as in the modern theatre, when the actor was to speak from a window, or balcony, or the walls of a fortress, the requisite ingenuity was not wanting to contrive a representation of the place. But with regard to the use of painted moveable scenery, it is not possible, from the very circumstances of the case, to believe him correct in his theory. Such a contrivance could not have escaped our ancestors. All the materials were ready to their hands. They had not to invent for themselves, but merely to adapt an old invention to that peculiar purpose; and at a time when every better-furnished apartment was adorned with tapestry; when even the rooms of the commonest taverns were hung with painted cloths; while all the materials were constantly before their eyes, we can hardly believe our forefathers to have been so deficient in ingenuity, as to have missed the simple contrivance of converting the common ornaments of their walls into the decorations of their theatres. But, in fact, the use of scenery was almost co-existent with the introduction of dramatic representations in this country. In the Chester Mysteries (1268), the most ancient and complete collection of the kind which we possess, is found the following stage direction: "Then Noe shall go into the arke with all his familye, his wife excepte. The arke must be boarded round about; and upon the boardes all the beastes and fowles, hereafter rehearsed, must be painted, that their wordes may agree with their pictures." In this passage we have a clear reference to a painted scene. It is not likely that, in the lapse of three centuries, while all other arts were in a state of rapid improvement, and the art of dramatic writing, perhaps, more rapidly and successfully improved than any other, the art of theatrical decoration should have alone stood still. It is not improbable that their scenes were few; and that they were varied, as occasion might require, by the introduction of different pieces of stage furniture. Mr. Gifford, who adheres to the opinions of Malone, says, "A table with a pen and ink thrust in, signified that the stage was a counting-house; if these were withdrawn and two stools put in their place, it was then a tavern." And this might be perfectly satisfactory as long as the business of the play was supposed to be passing within doors; but when it was removed to the open air, such meagre devices would no longer be sufficient to guide the imagination of the audience, and some new method must have been adopted to indicate the place of action. After giving the subject very considerable attention, I cannot help thinking that Steevens was right in rejecting Malone's theory, and concluding that the spectators were, as at the present day, assisted in following the progress of the story by means of painted moveable scenery. This opinion is confirmed by the ancient stage directions. In the folio Shakspeare, 1623, we read "Enter Brutus in his orchard; Enter Timon in the woods; Enter Timon from the cave." In Coriolanus, "Marcius follows them to the gates and is shut in." Innumerable instances of the same kind might be cited to prove that the ancient stage was not so defective in the necessary decorations as some antiquaries of great authority would represent. "It may be added," says Steevens, "that the dialogue of our old dramatists has such perpetual reference to objects supposed visible to the audience, that the want of scenery could not have failed to render many of the descriptions absurd. Banquo examines the outside of Inverness castle with such minuteness, that he distinguishes even the nests which the martens had built under the projecting part of its roof. Romeo, standing in a garden, points to the tops of fruit-trees gilded by the moon. The prologue speaker to the second part of Henry the Fourth expressly shows the spectators 'This worm-eaten hold of ragged stone,' in which Northumberland was lodged. Iachimo takes the most exact inventory of every article in Imogen's bed-chamber, from the silk and silver of which her tapestry was wrought, down to the Cupids that support her andirons. Had not the inside of the apartment, with its proper furniture, been represented, how ridiculous must the action of Iachimo have appeared! He must have stood looking out of the room for the particulars supposed to be visible within it." The works of Massinger would afford innumerable instances of a similar kind to vindicate the opinion which Steevens has asserted on the testimony of Shakspeare alone. But on this subject there is one passage which appears to me quite conclusive. Must not all the humour of the mock play in The Midsummer Night's Dream have been entirely lost, unless the audience before whom it was performed were accustomed to all the embellishments requisite to give effect to a dramatic representation, and could consequently estimate the absurdity of those shallow contrivances and mean substitutes for scenery devised by the ignorance of the clowns?

In only one respect do I perceive any material difference between the mode of representation at the time of Massinger and at present: in his day, the female parts were performed by boys. This custom, which must in many cases have materially injured the illusion of the scene, was in others of considerable advantage: it furnished the stage with a succession of youths, regularly educated for the art, to fill, in every department of the drama, the characters suited to their age. When the lad had become too tall for Juliet, he had acquired the skill, and was most admirably fitted, both in age and appearance, for performing the part which Garrick considered the most difficult on the stage, because it needed "an old head upon young shoulders," the ardent and arduous character of Romeo. When the voice had "the mannish crack," that rendered the youth unfit to appear as the representative of the gentle Imogen, the stage possessed in him the very person that was wanting to do justice to the princely sentiments of Arviragus or Guiderius.

Such was the state of the stage when Massinger arrived in the metropolis, and dedicated his talents to its service. He joined a splendid fraternity, for Shakspeare, Jonson, Beaumont, Fletcher, Shirley, were then flourishing at the height of their reputation, and the full vigour of their genius. Massinger came among them no unworthy competitor for such honours and emoluments as the theatre could afford. Of the honours, indeed, he seems to have reaped a very fair and equitable portion; of the emoluments, the harvest was less abundant. In those days, very little pecuniary reward was to be gained by the dramatic poet, unless, as indeed was most frequently the case, he added the profession of the actor to that of the author, and recited the verses which he wrote. The distinguished performers of that time, Alleyn, Burbage, Heminge, Condell, Shakspeare, all appear to have died in independent, if not affluent, circumstances; but the remuneration obtained by the poet was most miserably curtailed. The price given at the theatre for a new play fluctuated between ten and twenty pounds; the copyright, if the piece was printed, might produce from six to ten pounds more; in addition to these sums, the dedication-fee may be reckoned, the usual amount of which was forty shillings. Our author appears to have produced about two or three plays every year. Most of them were successful; but, even with this industry and good fortune, his annual income would rarely have exceeded fifty pounds: and we cannot, therefore, feel surprised at finding him continually speaking of his necessities; or that the only existing document connected with his life should be one that represents him in a state of pecuniary embarrassment.

Among the papers of Dulwich College, the indefatigable Mr. Malone discovered the following letter tripartite, which, coming from persons of such deserved celebrity, cannot fail of interesting the reader.

"To our most loving friend, Mr. Phillip Hinchlow, esquire, these.

"Mr. Hinchlow,

"You understand our unfortunate extremitie, and I doe not thincke you so void of Christianitie but that you would throw so much money into the Thames as wee request now of you, rather than endanger so many innocent lives. You know there is xl. more, at least, to be receaved of you for the play. We desire you to lend us vl. of that, which shall be allowed to you; without which, we cannot be bayled, nor I play any more till this be dispatch'd. It will lose you xxl. ere the end of the next weeke, besides the hindrance of the next new play. Pray, sir, consider our cases with humanity, and now give us cause to acknowledge you our true freind in time of neede. Wee have entreated Mr. Davison to deliver this note, as well to witness your love as our promises, and alwayes acknowledgement to be ever

"Your most thankfull and loving friends,
"NAT. FIELD."

"The money shall be abated out of the money remayns for the play of Mr. Fletcher and ours.
"ROB. DABORNE."

"I have ever found you a true loving friend to mee, and in soe small a suite, it beinge honest, I hope you will not fail us.
"PHILIP MASSINGER."

Indorsed.
"Received by mee, Robert Davison, of Mr. Hinchlow, for the use of Mr. Daboerne, Mr. Feeld, Mr. Messenger, the sum of vl.

The occasion of the distress in which these three distinguished persons were involved it is not possible to fathom. We may imagine a thousand emergencies, either creditable or discreditable to the fame of the writers, with which the letter would perfectly tally; but, on such slight and vague intimations, no ingenuity could determine which was most likely to be correct. But from the document a circumstance is ascertained, which, before its discovery, had been called in question. Sir Aston Cockayne, a friend of Massinger, had asserted in a volume of poems, published in 1658, that our author had written in conjunction with Fletcher; Davies doubted this report, but the above letter establishes the fact beyond the possibility of dispute.

Massinger is known to have produced thirty-seven plays for the stage, a list of which is given at the conclusion of this memoir. Sixteen entire plays and the fragment of another, The Parliament of Love, alone are extant. No less than eleven of his productions, in manuscript, were in possession of Mr. Warburton (Somerset Herald), and destroyed with the rest of that gentleman's invaluable collection by his cook, who, ignorant of their worth, used them as waste paper for the purposes of the kitchen.

The great and various merits of the works of Massinger will be better seen in the following volumes than in any elaborate, critical dissertation. If our author be compared with the other dramatic writers of his age, we cannot long hesitate where to place him. More natural in his characters and more poetical in his diction than Jonson or Cartwright, more elevated and nervous than Fletcher, the only writers who can be supposed to contest his pre-eminence, Massinger ranks immediately under Shakspeare himself. Our poet excels, perhaps, more in the description than in the expression of passion; this may in some measure be ascribed to his attention to the fable: while his scenes are managed with consummate skill, the lighter shades of character and sentiment are lost in the tendency of each part to the catastrophe. The melody, force, and variety of his versification are always remarkable. The prevailing beauties of his productions are dignity and elegance; their predominant fault is want of passion.

Massinger's last play—which is unfortunately lost—The Anchoress of Pausilippo, was acted Jan. 26, 1640, about six weeks before his death, which happened on the 17th of March, 1640. He went to bed in good health, says Langbaine, and was found dead in the morning, in his own house on the Bankside. He was buried in the churchyard of St. Saviour's, and the comedians paid the last sad duty to his name, by attending him to the grave.

It does not appear, though every stone and every fragment of a stone has been carefully examined, that any monument or inscription of any kind marked the place where his dust was deposited. "The memorial of his mortality," says Gifford, "is given with a pathetic brevity, which accords but too well with the obscure and humble passages of his life: March 20, 1639-40, buried Philip Massinger, A STRANGER."

Such is all the information that remains to us of this distinguished poet. But though we are ignorant of every circumstance respecting him but that he lived, wrote, and died, we may yet form some idea of his personal character from the recommendatory poems prefixed to his several plays, in which, as Mr. Gifford justly observes, the language of his panegyrists, though warm, expresses an attachment apparently derived not so much from his talents as his virtues: he is their beloved, much-esteemed, dear, worthy, deserving, honoured, long-known, and long-loved friend. All the writers of his life represent him as a man of singular modesty, gentleness, candour, and affability; nor does it appear that he ever made or found an enemy.

As would be expected many works from this time not longer exist either in part or their entirety. Further many playwrights collaborated on plays or revised them for later performances and we have used the latest position known on each of them for the bibliography below..

Solo Plays
The Maid of Honour, tragicomedy (c. 1621; printed 1632)
The Duke of Milan, tragedy (c. 1621–3; printed 1623, 1638)
The Unnatural Combat, tragedy (c. 1621–6; printed 1639)
The Bondman, tragicomedy (licensed 3 December 1623; printed 1624)
The Renegado, tragicomedy (licensed 17 April 1624; printed 1630)
The Parliament of Love, comedy (licensed 3 November 1624; MS)
A New Way to Pay Old Debts, comedy (c. 1625; printed 1632)
The Roman Actor, tragedy (licensed 11 October 1626; printed 1629)
The Great Duke of Florence, tragicomedy (licensed 5 July 1627; printed 1636)
The Picture, tragicomedy (licensed 8 June 1629; printed 1630)
The Emperor of the East, tragicomedy (licensed 11 March 1631; printed 1632)
Believe as You List, tragedy (rejected by the censor in January, but licensed 6 May 1631; MS)
The City Madam, comedy (licensed 25 May 1632; printed 1658)
The Guardian, comedy (licensed 31 October 1633; printed 1655)
The Bashful Lover, tragicomedy (licensed 9 May 1636; printed 1655)

Collaborations with John Fletcher
Sir John van Olden Barnavelt, tragedy (August 1619; MS)
The Little French Lawyer, comedy (c. 1619–23; printed 1647)
A Very Woman, tragicomedy (c. 1619–22; licensed 6 June 1634; printed 1655)
The Custom of the Country, comedy (c. 1619–23; printed 1647)
The Double Marriage, tragedy (c. 1619–23; Printed 1647)
The False One, history (c. 1619–23; printed 1647)
The Prophetess, tragicomedy (licensed 14 May 1622; printed 1647)
The Sea Voyage, comedy (licensed 22 June 1622; printed 1647)
The Spanish Curate, comedy (licensed 24 October 1622; printed 1647)
The Lovers' Progress or The Wandering Lovers, tragicomedy (licensed Dec 1623; rev 1634; printed 1647)
The Elder Brother, comedy (c. 1625; printed 1637).

Collaborations with John Fletcher and Francis Beaumont
Thierry and Theodoret, tragedy (c. 1607; printed 1621)
The Coxcomb, comedy (1608–10; printed 1647)
Beggars' Bush, comedy (c. 1612–15; revised 1622; printed 1647)
Love's Cure, comedy (c. 1612–15; revised 1625; printed 1647).

Collaborations with John Fletcher and Nathan Field
The Honest Man's Fortune, tragicomedy (1613; printed 1647)
The Queen of Corinth, tragicomedy (c. 1616–18; printed 1647)

The Knight of Malta, tragicomedy (c. 1619; printed 1647).

Collaborations with Nathan Field
The Fatal Dowry, tragedy (c. 1619, printed 1632); adapted by Nicholas Rowe: The Fair Penitent

Collaborations with John Fletcher, John Ford, and William Rowley, or John Webster
The Fair Maid of the Inn, comedy (licensed 22 January 1626; printed 1647).

Collaborations with John Fletcher, Ben Jonson, and George Chapman
Rollo Duke of Normandy, or The Bloody Brother, tragedy (c. 1616–24; printed 1639).

Collaborations with Thomas Dekker
The Virgin Martyr, tragedy (licensed 6 October 1620; printed 1622).

Collaborations with Thomas Middleton and William Rowley
The Old Law, comedy (c. 1615–18; printed 1656).

www.ingramcontent.com/pod-product-compliance
Lightning Source LLC
Chambersburg PA
CBHW060132050426
42448CB00010B/2078